MW01701620

Queensland

Art Gallery

Collection

Souvenir

A Queensland Art Gallery Publication

Publisher
Queensland Art Gallery
Queensland Cultural Centre
South Brisbane

PO Box 3686
South Brisbane
Queensland 4101
Australia

All possible care has been taken to ensure that the colour reproductions match as closely as possible the colour transparencies of the original works of art.

National Library of Australia
Cataloguing-in-Publication data

Queensland Art Gallery
Queensland Art Gallery: souvenir

Includes index.
ISBN 0 7242 4841.2.

1. Queensland Art Gallery—Catalogs. 2. Art museums—Queensland—Brisbane—Catalogs. 3. Art, Australian—Queensland—Brisbane—Catalogs. 4. Art—Queensland—Brisbane—Catalogs. I. —. II. Title.

708.99431

The following abbreviations have been used: c.: circa or about; cm: centimetre; diam.: diameter; irreg.: irregular; comp.: composition.

Dimensions of works are given in centimetres (cm), height preceding width, followed by depth.

Cover
William Robinson
Dark tide, Bogangar 1994

Acknowledgments
The Gallery thanks the following copyright owners who gave permission to reproduce gratis:

Gordon Bennett—*Triptych: Requiem, Of Grandeur, Empire*
Peter Blum—Louise Bourgeois, *Sainte Sébastienne*
Arthur Boyd—*Bathers and Pulpit Rock*
Helen Brack—John Brack, *Finale*
Felix Bunduk—Nym Bunduk, *Nakymal painting*
Alison Clouston—*Pterodactyl car*
William Delafield Cook—*A haystack*
David Thomas—Grace Crowley, *(Abstract)*
Dolly Nampijinpa Daniels—*Bush Grain Dreaming*
Aleks Danko—*Day in day out (second version)*
Juan Davila—*Miss Sigmund*
Claudia Gian Ferrari—Leonardo Dudreville, *Expansion of poetry*
Judi Elliott—*Platter: ... of how things are*
Gilbert & George—*Leaners*
Elvin Harvey & Revs Bruce and David Harvey Noble—L. J. Harvey, *Wallbracket: Infancy, Youth and Maturity*
Emily Kame Kngwarreye—*Wild Potato Dreaming*
Colin Lanceley, Mike Brown—Brown, Crothal, Lanceley, *The Café Balzac mural*
Helen Levitt—*(Untitled)*
Mary Morris, Marlborough Gallery Inc.—Jacques Lipchitz, *Musical instruments*
Allan M. Wight—Sydney Long, *Spirit of the Plains*
Richard Long—*Ring of stones*
Bea Maddock—*Square*
The Uniting Church in Australia, Queensland Synod & Surf Life Saving Queensland Inc.—Daphne Mayo, *The Olympian*
Ottie Molvig Bartzis—Jon Molvig, *A twilight of women*
Lady Nolan—Sidney Nolan, *Mrs Fraser*
Bronwyn Oliver—*Curlicue*
Glen O'Malley—*Sideburn scramble*
Mimmo Paladino—*Canto notturno (Night song)*
Mike Parr—*Wax wedge (the trinity of bones)*
John Perceval—*Sculpture: The Herald Angel*
Thea Waddell—Thea Proctor, *The swing*
Robert Rooney—*Kind-hearted kitchen-garden I*
Bernard Sachs—*During philosophy—group portrait with head*
Gordon Shepherdson—*Man climbing over images*
Artes Magnus—Cindy Sherman, *Madame de Pompadour née Poisson (1721–1764)*
Rodney Spooner—*Civilised obsession*
Kathy Temin—*White problem #2*
Rover Thomas—*Barramundi Dreaming*
Joe Tilson—*Ho Chi Minh*
Shigeo Toya—*Woods III*
Jane Starey—Jessie Traill, *Beautiful victims*
Albert Tucker—*Study for 'Images of modern evil: Spring in Fitzroy'*
Judith Murray—Roland Wakelin, *The Bridge under construction*

Contents

The Queensland Art Gallery and Collection 4

Australian Art to 1965 10

Contemporary Australian Art 50

International Art 92

Index to artists 136

The Queensland Art Gallery and Collection

The Queensland Art Gallery opened on its present site on the banks of the Brisbane River in June 1982. The opening celebrations looked to the Gallery's future, but they also drew to a close a period of eighty-seven years during which the Gallery's role and functions were consistently limited by a succession of premises with few institutional resources. While also marking the beginning of the splendid Queensland Cultural Centre, this new permanent facility enabled the creation of a radically expanded program, a more certain foundation for the State Collection and spectacular growth in the Gallery's audience.

Appropriately, the first moves to establish an Art Gallery in Queensland were driven by artists. In 1883 the recently arrived English artist Isaac Walter Jenner petitioned the colonial Government to provide the necessary resources. Jenner's plea was treated with indifference. Nevertheless he maintained his enthusiasm and in 1887 founded the Queensland Art Society. Several years later Godfrey Rivers, President of the Society and an influential art instructor at the Brisbane Technical College, revived public interest in the issue. Rivers persuaded the Mayor of Brisbane, Robert Fraser, to make available a room in the then Town Hall building. A number of prominent citizens lent works of art, artists such as Jenner and Rivers made generous donations of their own work, and these, along with a bequest of seventeenth-century Dutch paintings from the estate of politician and pastoralist the Hon. T. L. Murray-Prior, formed the nucleus of the first Collection.

The Gallery was officially opened by the Governor, Sir Henry Wylie Norman, on 29 March 1895. It was managed by a Board of Trustees under the distinguished chairmanship of Sir Samuel Griffith, Chief Justice of Queensland. Godfrey Rivers served as Honorary Curator from 1895 to 1914. The first purchase by the new Gallery, in 1896, was the sentimental Victorian genre painting *Evicted* 1887, by the British artist

Opposite
Exterior views of the Queensland Art Gallery

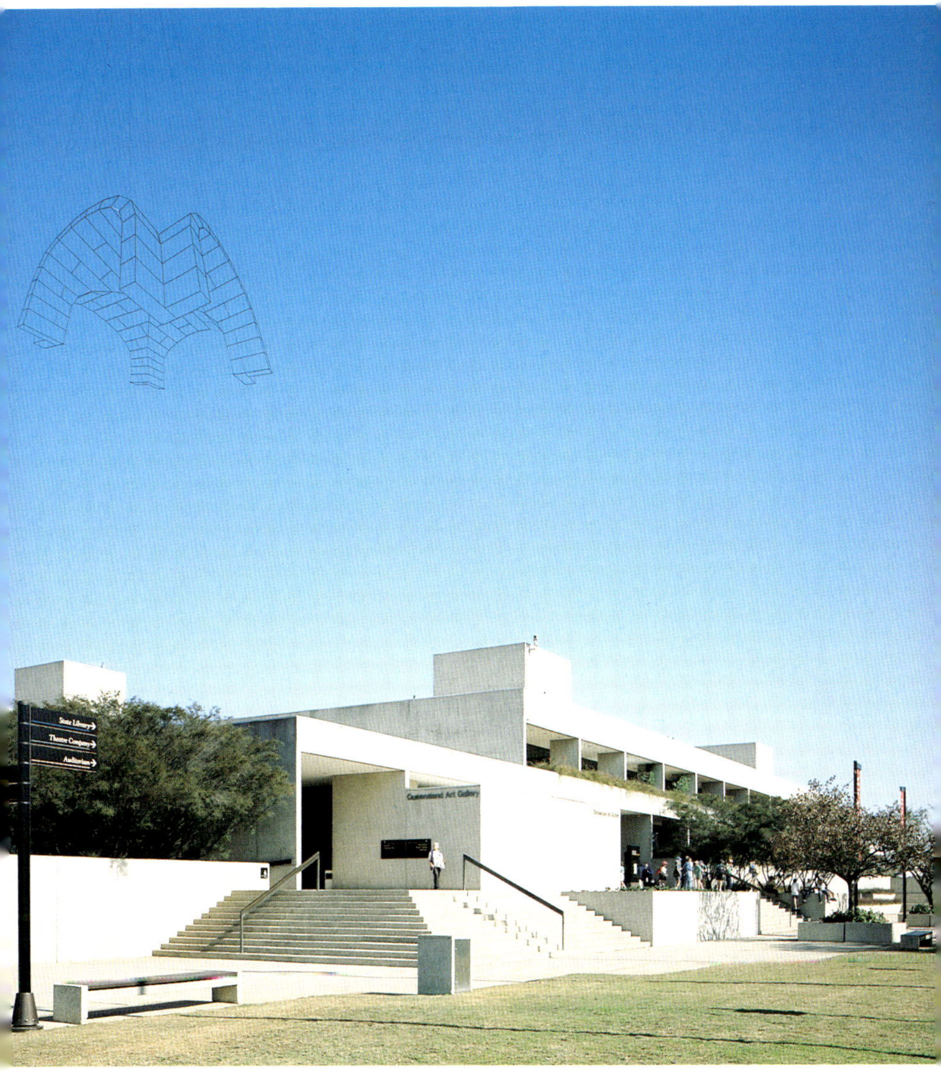
State Library
Theatre Company
Auditorium
Queensland Art Gallery

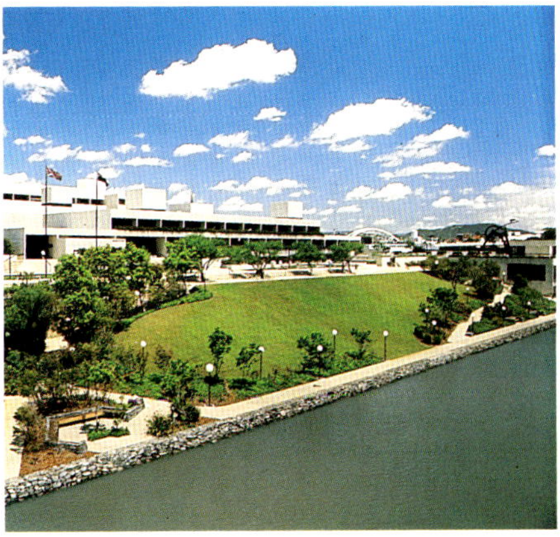

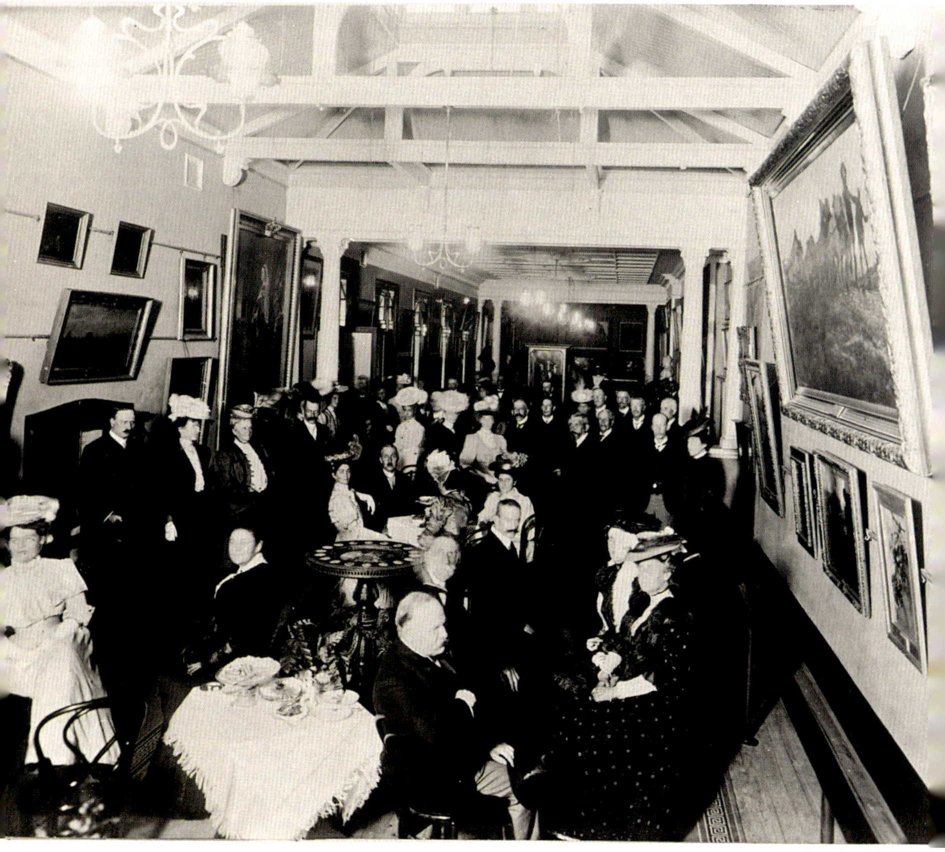

Blandford Fletcher. This work remains one of the most popular in the Collection. The first Australian work purchased, in 1898, was Josephine Muntz-Adams's *Care* 1897, also one of the Gallery's popular works.

For several decades the history of the Gallery was marked by periods of enthusiasm and some important acquisitions, but the path to true consolidation was blocked by a lack of funding and moves to a succession of inadequate premises. Momentum to establish a new permanent facility gathered in the late 1960s and coincided with major changes in the nation's cultural landscape. During this period cultural life began to be seen as an essential indicator of the sophisticated quality of Australian life, and the arts became a priority for governments and communities.

In November 1968 the eminent Australian art historian Professor Bernard Smith judged the H. C. Richards Memorial Prize at the Gallery, and in his address to the audience described the state of the visual arts in Queensland as 'weedy and malnourished'. His speech generated much media attention and was the focus of debate for several weeks. That same year the Trustees of the Gallery made a submission to the State Government which told of the Collection's desperate need for adequate accommodation. At last there was action. A Special Committee was established, a site chosen, and within a few years the project had expanded to include an impressive and comprehensive cultural complex housing the Art Gallery, the State Library, the Queensland Museum and a venue for the Performing Arts.

This complex now operates as the effective cornerstone of Queensland cultural life. Architecturally, the Queensland Art Gallery is the most acclaimed building of its type in Australia. The symmetry and coherence of its interior spaces are ideally suited to the display and enjoyment of all forms of art.

Opposite
The Queensland Art Gallery Collection in the former Queensland Government Executive Building, 1907 (now an international hotel)

With the move to the South Bank site, the Gallery's programs began to focus on the support of touring temporary exhibitions and the provision of services to regional Queensland. The Gallery at this time functioned largely as an institution receiving exhibitions, with a program that fully engaged the possibilities offered by its award-winning architecture. However, with its institutional resources considerably expanded, the Gallery soon achieved an international reputation for the innovative and professional presentation of exhibitions and of its own Collection. This recognition has resulted in the Gallery's outstanding success in the organisation of major international exhibitions such as 'Matisse' (1995), 'Treasures from the Shanghai Museum' (1990) and 'Masterpieces from the Louvre: French Bronzes and Paintings from the Renaissance to Rodin' (1988).

In recent years the Collection has grown at a rate of approximately 350 works per year. From some 4000 works in 1982, by early 1996 it totalled almost 10 000, covering all media and including paintings, sculpture, installations, decorative arts, prints, drawings and photographs. Early twentieth-century and modern Australian and international collection areas are also being further developed in ways which allow the 'telling' of specific art histories and contextualise works already in the Collection. The Collection not only reflects the full range of contemporary Australian art, but also demonstrates the Gallery's commitment to Queensland-based art, the art of Aboriginal and Torres Strait Islander peoples, and that of the Asia-Pacific region.

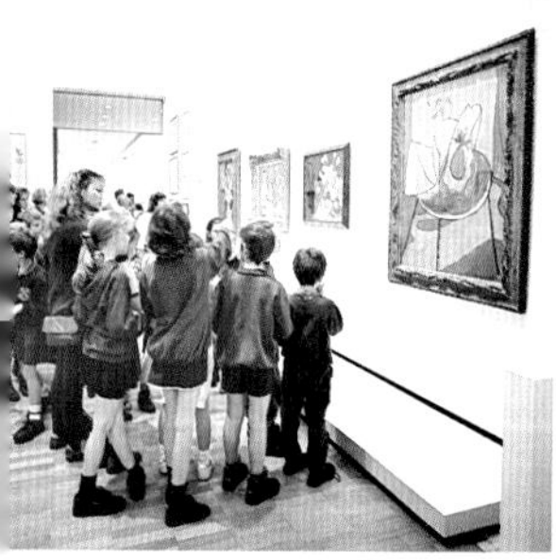

A school group touring the 'Matisse' exhibition, 1995

The Gallery 14 project space, with its emphasis on contemporary installation work, increases the visibility of and access to new and challenging art practices. Through its visiting artist-in-residence programs, scholarly forums, floor talks and lectures by artists, and the allocation of studio scholarships to young and emerging local artists, the Oueensland Art Gallery acknowledges the crucial relationship between practitioners and their public.

The Gallery's rapid development of significant links with the Asia-Pacific region and the increasing representation of its many cultures within the Collection reflect the ways in which

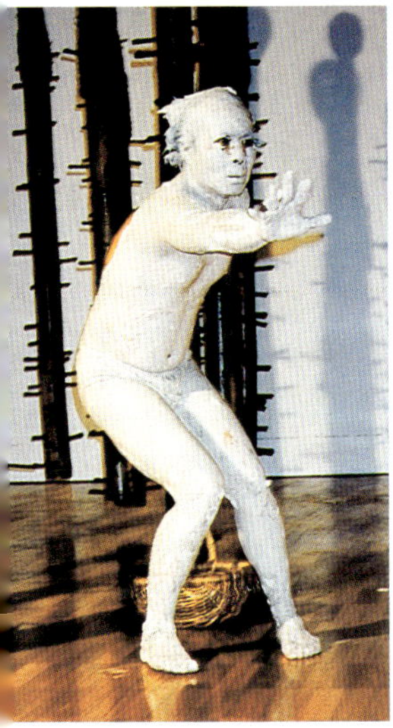

Indonesian artist Dadang Christanto in performance at the 'First Asia-Pacific Triennial of Contemporary Art' 1993

Australia as a whole is seeking to better understand and 'locate' itself within the region. Through its major exhibition initiative, the Asia-Pacific Triennial of Contemporary Art, the Gallery has helped to form important collaborative structures for this 'search for meaning', and the dialogue and exchange achieved will continue into the twenty-first century.

The Queensland Art Gallery has long abandoned the notion of the museum as a cultural storehouse, a solemn container of collective (and selective) memory. The Gallery acknowledges in its programs and policies that visitors receive far more from exhibitions than just information about the objects displayed. Visiting an art gallery is a complex experience involving architecture, light and space, and the varied presentation of art objects. Within both Collection and temporary exhibition displays, the Gallery offers a range of interpretive materials and events, including workshops, performances, seminars and publications, which contribute to a continual reassessment and redefinition of the cultural life of Queensland.

Australian Art to 1965

The Queensland Art Gallery's largest permanent display component is the Australian art collection and it has assumed a highly diverse character since its formative years, during which the emphasis was on painting, sculpture and works on paper. While colonial painting forms a comparatively small part of the Australian collection, the Gallery nevertheless holds major works by late nineteenth-century Queensland artists such as Isaac Walter Jenner and Godfrey Rivers, as well as work in media as varied as stained glass, jewellery and photography. In many instances these works have a specific relationship with Queensland, either as a site of production or as a point of historic reference.

The nineteenth-century decorative arts collection reflects the widespread use of native flora and fauna as emblems of a developing nationalism. Depictions of kangaroos, emus, brolgas, possums, snakes, lizards, cockatoos, ferns and fruit appeared in jewellery, furniture, stained glass and other decorative art objects. The ready availability of emu eggs saw them mounted as cups, caskets and desk sets, similar to the use of ostrich eggs in renaissance Europe.

While many local artists had earlier wrestled with the concept of a distinctly 'Australian' landscape tradition, this sentiment found its greatest expression with the advent of the Heidelberg School, represented in the collection by several works by Arthur Streeton, Frederick McCubbin, Charles Conder and Walter Withers. These works well describe the interest of these artists in mood and light and in capturing the 'impression' of a moment.

Towards the end of the century, when the expectation of Federation of the colonies became even stronger, specific images of Australian life began to appear both locally and in English items created especially for this market. The stained glass window commissioned by James Finney for his house in Brisbane is particularly noteworthy. The English Arts and Crafts movement, inspired by the writings of William Morris, also began to have its influence from the 1890s. L.J. Harvey in Brisbane produced works in which native fauna and flora, especially gum leaves and nuts, proliferated. Harvey, who trained as a woodcarver and modeller, exhibited small sculptural pieces in exhibitions of the Royal Queensland Art Society. He combined both these skills when he began to teach hand-built pottery at the Central Technical College from 1916 and devised a unique series of exercises which readily identifies the work of his many students.

The collection contains several major works of the symbolist movement by Sydney Long, Bernard Hall and Arthur Loureiro. Long's enchanting *Spirit of the Plains* 1897 perhaps best describes the fusing of classical mythology with a distinctly Australian character. An expressive silhouette of gum trees became a hallmark of Australian art nouveau. This is especially evident in the background of this painting as well as in Jessie Traill's etching *Beautiful victims* 1914. A similar character is also found in many of the works of the watercolourist J.J. Hilder.

The Australian art collection includes work by Australian-born, expatriate, and immigrant artists, and artists who worked here only briefly. Work by Australians who in the late nineteenth and early twentieth centuries, largely or in part, located their practices in Europe are particularly strong. Through these paintings, by artists such as Rupert Bunny, George Lambert, E. Phillips Fox and John Peter Russell, the stresses or benefits of expatriation on an artist's career can be investigated.

Russell's *Roc Toul* 1911, strongly influenced by his impressionist contacts, was one of a number of works to come into the collection through the donations of Sir Leon and Lady Trout. Bunny is represented by several works such as the massively-scaled *Bathers* 1906 and later paintings which indicate his borrowing of vivid Fauvist colours, such as *Echo and Narcissus* c.1914–19. Both the *fin de siècle* decorative arts and Australian holdings have been enhanced considerably by the acquisition of a silk and mahogany screen painted by Charles Conder in Paris in 1899.

Vida Lahey trained at the National Gallery School, Melbourne during 1905–09 and absorbed the figurative style of her teacher Bernard Hall. *Monday morning* 1912, painted three years after she left the school and one of the Gallery's most popular works, is the only known survivor of a group of large-scale figurative works, some of which were destroyed in a studio fire. Lahey later made several trips to Europe where she was influenced by modernism. Her popular and colourful floral still lifes helped establish her reputation.

A bronze cast of the Daphne Mayo sculpture *The Olympian* c.1946, cast after 1958, celebrates another distinguished Queensland woman artist who played a significant role in the development of the Gallery and of the local art scene. In the Gallery's centenary year, the casting of Mayo's *Susannah* was supported by the Queensland Art Gallery Society.

These works, and others by artists such as Margaret Preston, Hilda Rix-Nicholas, A. M. E. Bale, Grace Cossington Smith, Grace Crowley and Margaret Cilento, allow very focused study on the role of women within the Australian art system. Many of these works describe the crucial relationship between women practitioners and the development of modernism in this country. For instance Margaret Preston was one of the first Australian artists to realise the unique value of Aboriginal art, distinguished as it was by earthy colours and flat patterning, later inspiring such works as *Aboriginal still life* 1940.

Around this time Albert Namatjira was taught watercolour painting by the Melbourne artist Rex Battarbee. Namatjira's work accorded with the regionalist style established by Hans Heysen in South Australia and, consequently, his first exhibition in 1938 quickly sold out and created a fashion for his work. Though disparaged by the art intelligentsia of the time, his paintings are now regarded as having specific links with his tribal lands. While holdings of Aboriginal art are small before 1980, the collection includes some examples of outstanding quality, such as *Nakymal painting (Muriia-Potha totemic landscape)* c.1959–60 by Nym Bunduk, and several significant bark paintings which were gifted to the Gallery

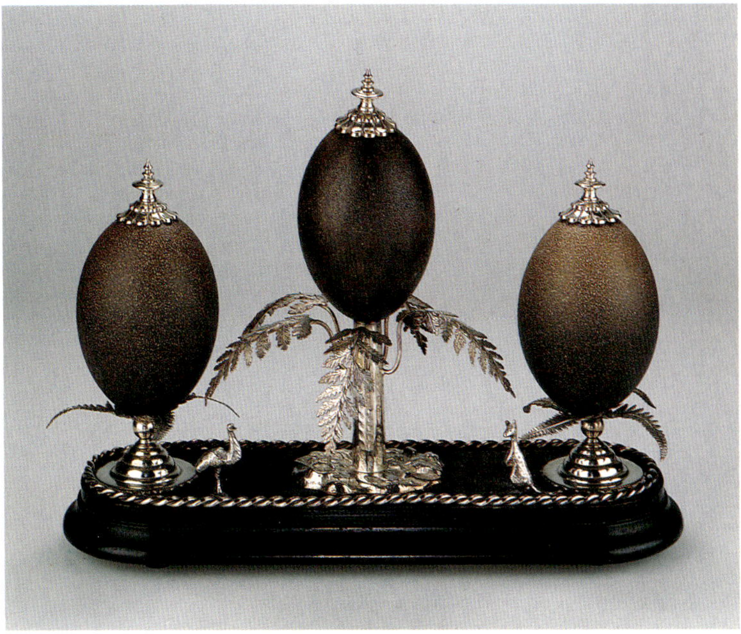

Above
Evan Jones (attrib. to)
Australia NSW 1846–1917
Table decoration c.1865
Stirling silver and emu eggs
31.7 x 40 x 12cm
Gift of Mr W.S. Moore 1971

Right
William Edwards (attrib. to)
Australia Vic. c.1819–c.1889
Racing trophy: The Wythes and Hodgson Cup c.1870–73
Cast and modelled stirling silver
51 x 15cm (with base)
Gift of Miss Pamela Bell 1985

The Wythes and Hodgson Cup *was originally awarded at the 1873 Hill End Annual Races. The trophy was subsequently purchased in Sydney in 1903 by the donor's grandfather for presentation at the Lyndhurst Amateur Race Club in the Gulf of Carpentaria. The cup is unmarked, but is attributed to William Edwards of Melbourne, as the embossed racing scene and decorative details are representative of that firm's work.* The Table decoration *is a commercial production, incorporating the nationalistic symbol of the kangaroo and emu.*

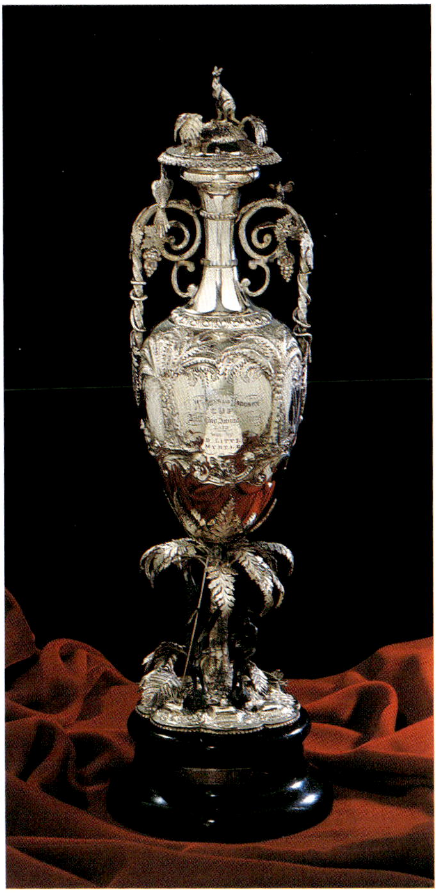

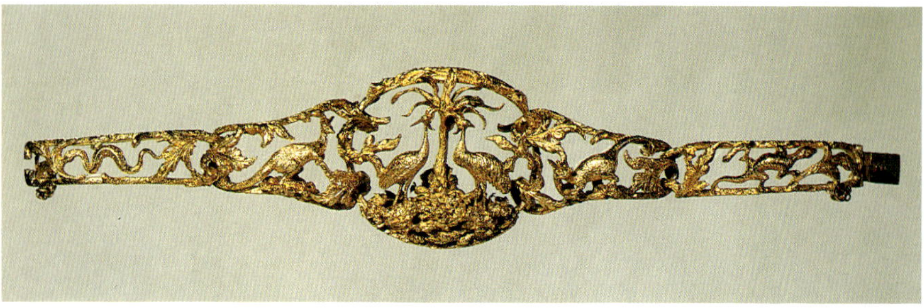

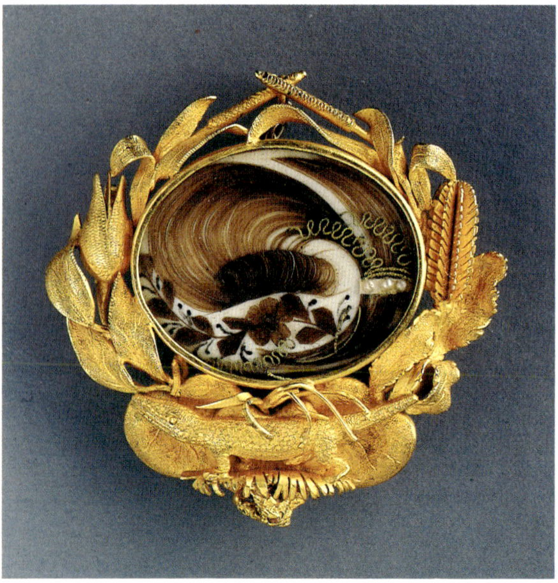

Above
Unknown
Australia
Bracelet 1864
Modelled gold
3.8 x 17 x 1 cm
Purchased 1987. Queensland Art Gallery Foundation

Left
Hogarth, Erichsen & Co.
Australia c.1854–c.1965
Julius Hogarth
Australia NSW unknown
Conrad Erichsen
Australia NSW unknown
Mourning brooch c.1860
Gold, hair, silk and pearls
5.8 x 5.6 x 1.3 cm
Gift of Mrs Alison Forster 1990

Most of the jewellery worn in Australia during the nineteenth century was manufactured in Birmingham. The Australian pieces made by firms such as Hogarth, Erichsen & Co. are distinctive in their use of native flora and fauna. This brooch is connected with the Archer family of Gracemere, outside Rockhampton, and includes a waterlily and goanna motif and a small gold nugget. Although the identity of the maker of the bracelet is unknown, it is thought to have been made in the Victorian goldfields. The rusticated frames and details of the cast birds and animals indicate considerable skill.

in 1956 following the 1948 American-Australian Scientific Expedition to Arnhem Land, led by the anthropologist Charles Mountford.

The purchase of a major work by Roland Wakelin, *The Bridge under construction* 1928, further strengthened the Gallery's group of works by Sydney-based early modernists. The collection also includes a fine group of paintings and drawings by Sydney-born Eric Wilson. Wilson, who studied at Amédée Ozenfant's Academy in London and was exposed to the paintings of Braque and Leger, painted *The violin* 1939 before securing passage to Australia, and *Stove theme* 1942 on the verso after his return. Another work from the 1940s, *The Cypriot* 1940, shows Archibald Prize winner William Dobell's mastery of character through the psychological observation of the sitter.

George Bell, whose art school was established in Melbourne in 1932, became a major proponent of modernist ideas and had a profound influence on many young artists. Sali Herman, Russell Drysdale and Peter Purves Smith were amongst his most important students. Purves Smith travelled to Europe with Drysdale and they were among the few Australian artists to be influenced by surrealism. Purves Smith died shortly after the Second World War. His painting, *The Nazis, Nuremberg* 1938 is the major example of his small output. Drysdale, on the other hand, had a long and distinguished career, becoming famous for his scenes of life in the outback. His vision of the Australian landscape was directly counter to that of the Heidelberg School and the conventions of the 'Golden Summer'. *Bush fire* 1944 is at once harsh and familiar and, as a body of work, his landscapes are original and challenging.

Depictions of working life were the exception in Australian art until a group of social realist artists, Josl Bergner, Victor O'Connor and Noel Counihan, began their careers in Melbourne from the mid 1930s. Themes were focused on the economic depression of the period, on poverty and the dispossessed. These artists grew to be fierce critics of capitalism. In Sydney, the documentary photographs of Max Dupain during the 1940s often addressed social concerns and he is well represented in the collection.

Working concurrently in Melbourne during the 1940s was the group of artists who came to be known as the 'Angry Penguins'—Sidney Nolan, Arthur Boyd, Albert Tucker and John Perceval. Their work was significantly more personal than the political art of Noel Counihan and the social realists. It eschewed traditional links with the art of the past, instead concentrating on the significance of 'vitality' in art. Nolan consistently pursued some Australian historical narratives—the stories of bushranger Ned Kelly, the shipwrecked Mrs Fraser and the 1915 Gallipoli campaign—which have since taken on a mythological dimension in Australian cultural life. The Queensland Art Gallery Centenary Acquisitions Fund has allowed purchases of major works by some of these artists.

An artist whose work is distinctively individual was the British-born Ian Fairweather. Trained at the Slade School, London in 1920–24, Fairweather was, for the last twenty years of his life, a resident on Queensland's Bribie Island. Appropriately, Fairweather is well represented with important works such as *Epiphany* 1962, *Kite flying* 1958 and *War and Peace* 1959. These works were painted in a period of intense and productive activity, with the artist often working on as many as six or seven paintings at once.

While abstract expressionism took hold elsewhere, figuration continued to dominate in the work of later Melbourne-based artists. Charles Blackman, Arthur Boyd, Robert Dickerson and Clifton Pugh were all signatories to the 1959 'Antipodean Manifesto', which was anti-abstraction and which attempted to define the basic precepts of artistic meaning for Australian artists and audiences. Although Queensland-based Jon Molvig's figurative expressionist paintings reflected these concerns, he resolutely refused to join the 'antipodeans'. The debates that were prevalent at this time about which artistic idiom best suited the Australian

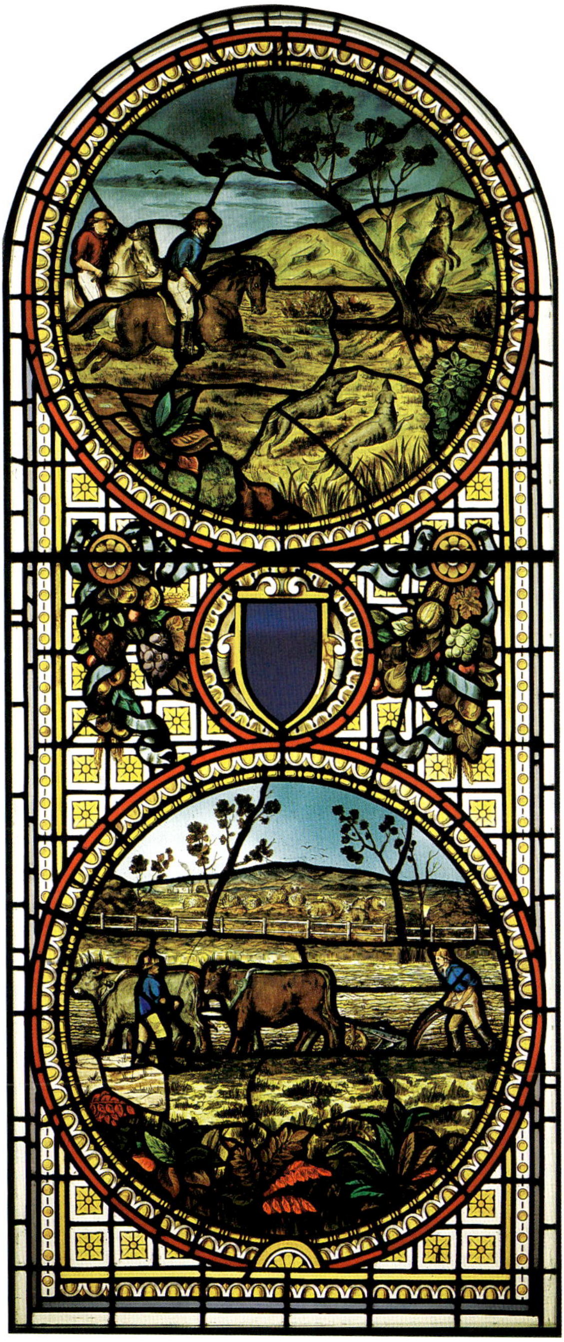

Unknown
Ireland
Stained glass window
c.1882
Stained and leaded glass
204 x 88cm
Gift of the Australian Broadcasting Corporation, Brisbane 1988

This window is the only known nineteenth-century stained glass in Australia to include a depiction of a kangaroo hunt. The portrayal of an ox-drawn plough is almost as uncommon. A third panel depicting a duck-hunting expedition was originally included below. The window was imported from Ireland in 1882 for use in Sydney House, Toowong, now the site of the ABC studios.

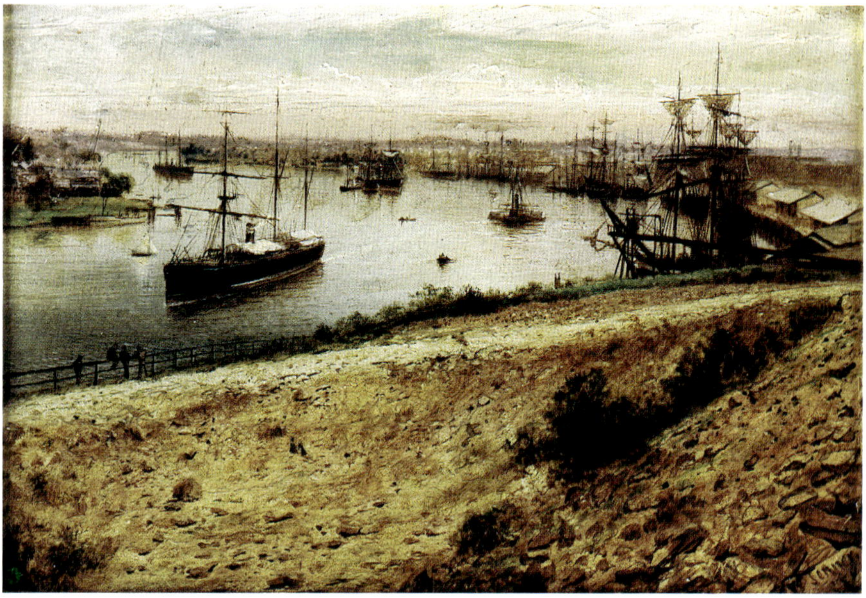

Isaac Walter Jenner
England/Australia 1836–1902
Brisbane from Bowen Terrace, New Farm 1888
Oil on board
14.5 x 21.8cm
Purchased 1995. Queensland Art Gallery Foundation

In Jenner's Brisbane from Bowen Terrace, New Farm *the meticulous detail of the painting, in particular the rigging of the ship, attest to the artist's earlier career in the British navy. The main ship in the painting is the RMS* Quetta, *which was regularly used on the London–Brisbane ocean mail service. A photograph of a similar view appeared in a local paper in 1895. In 1890, two years after Jenner completed this painting, the* Quetta *sank in Torres Strait. The Story Bridge, rather than ships' masts, now dominates this skyline.*

experience had their quirkiest expression in the work of the so-called Annandale Imitation Realists—Mike Brown, Ross Crothall and Colin Lancely. These artists worked collaboratively in a style which borrowed from, and destabilised, several established trends, including expressionism, pop art, primitive art and dada.

The Gallery's goal with the Australian art collection is to relate and display those narratives, some still evolving through scholarship, which are crucial to an understanding of Australian art history. The works featured in this publication do not, of course, tell the whole story, but they do represent some highlights—popular and cultural—for your enjoyment.

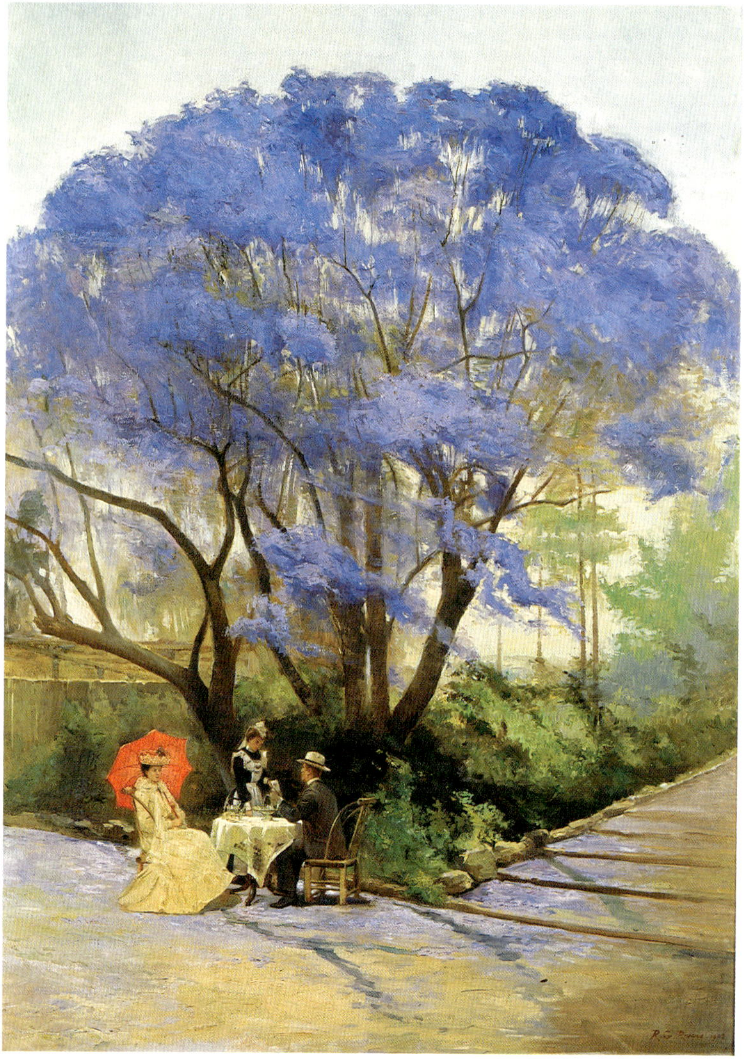

R. Godfrey Rivers
England/Australia 1859–1925
Under the jacaranda 1903
Oil on canvas
143.4 x 107.2cm
Purchased 1903

Godfrey Rivers taught at Brisbane's Central Technical College from 1890 to 1915, making the adjoining City Botanic Gardens a popular outdoor painting and sketching location. The jacaranda tree in this painting was probably one of the first grown in Australia. Seeds for the native South American tree were brought to Brisbane in 1864, and 50 000 seeds and cuttings had been distributed in Queensland by 1875. Godfrey Rivers has captured the beauty of the tree in full bloom, its carpet of mauve now a recognisable sight in Brisbane in the warmer months.

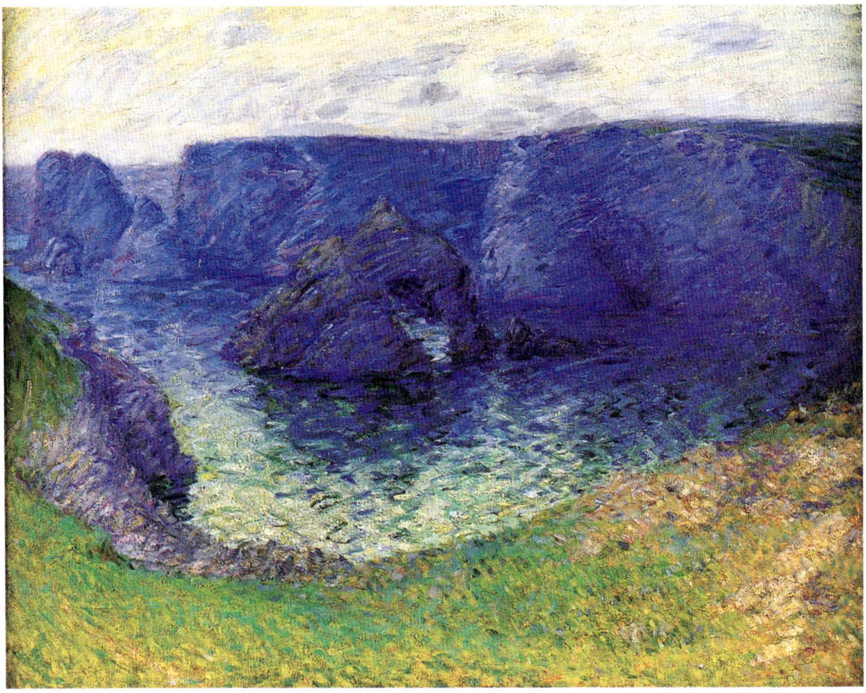

John Peter Russell
Australia/France 1859–1930
Roc Toul 1911
Oil on canvas
98.4 x 128cm
Gift of Lady Trout 1979

Sydney-born Russell spent most of his artistic life in France, where he first embraced impressionism. As a student in Paris in 1885, he met and worked with Toulouse-Lautrec, Rodin, and Van Gogh before settling on Belle-Ile, off the coast of Brittany, in 1886. On Belle-Ile, Russell developed a friendship with Claude Monet and the pair painted numerous landscapes of the dramatic coastline. Typical of Russell's Belle-Ile works, Roc Toul *displays the sketch-like use of pure colour characteristic of his impressionist style.*

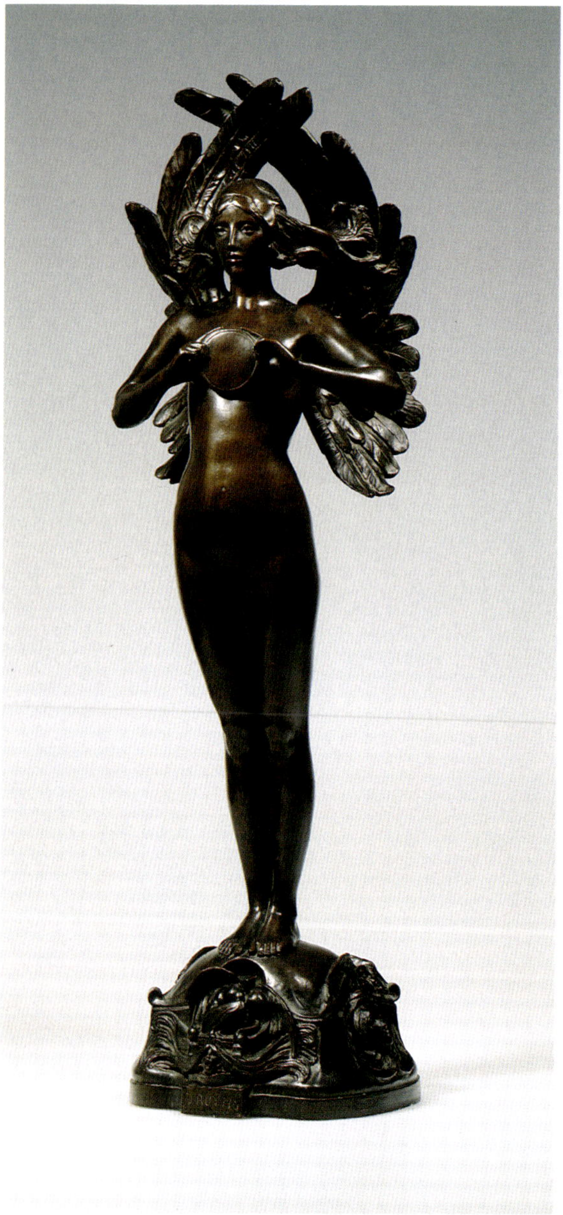

Bertram Mackennal
Australia/England 1863–1931
Truth 1894
Bronze
62 x 19.5 x 17.5cm
Purchased 1989 from the estate of Lady Trout with a special allocation from the Queensland Government

Bertram Mackennal reached a level of international acclaim previously unknown to an Australian artist, being the first to be elected to the Royal Academy and to be knighted. The son of sculptor John Mackennal, he studied classical statuary in the British Museum while attending the Royal Academy School. Mackennal became well known for his expressive yet graceful sculptures which encapsulate the spirit of the age.

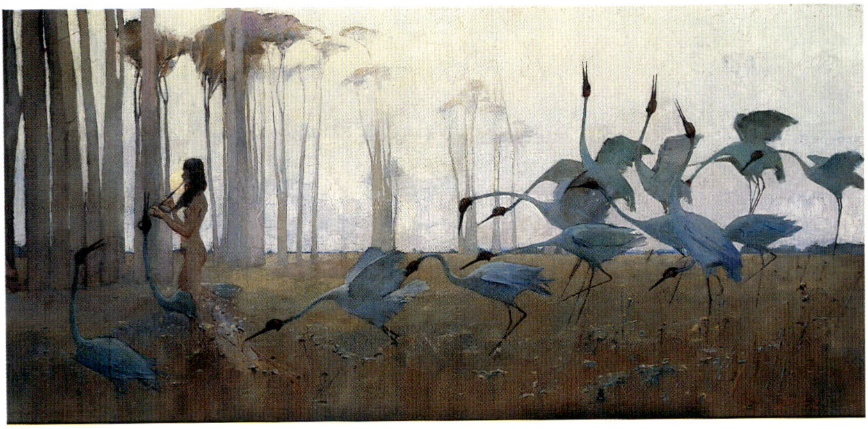

Sydney Long
Australia NSW 1871–1955
Spirit of the Plains 1897
Oil on canvas on wood
62 x 131.4cm
Gift of William Howard-Smith
in memory of his grandfather,
Ormond Charles Smith, 1940

Long was one of the first Australian artists to successfully combine classical mythology with a distinctly Australian landscape. As a protégé and then colleague of the influential Australian artist Julian Ashton, Long developed a style which enveloped the Australian bush in a poetic, pagan fantasy. This new bush lyricism, of which Spirit of the Plains *is a major example, brought Long much popularity and sufficient success for him to study in England for several years.*

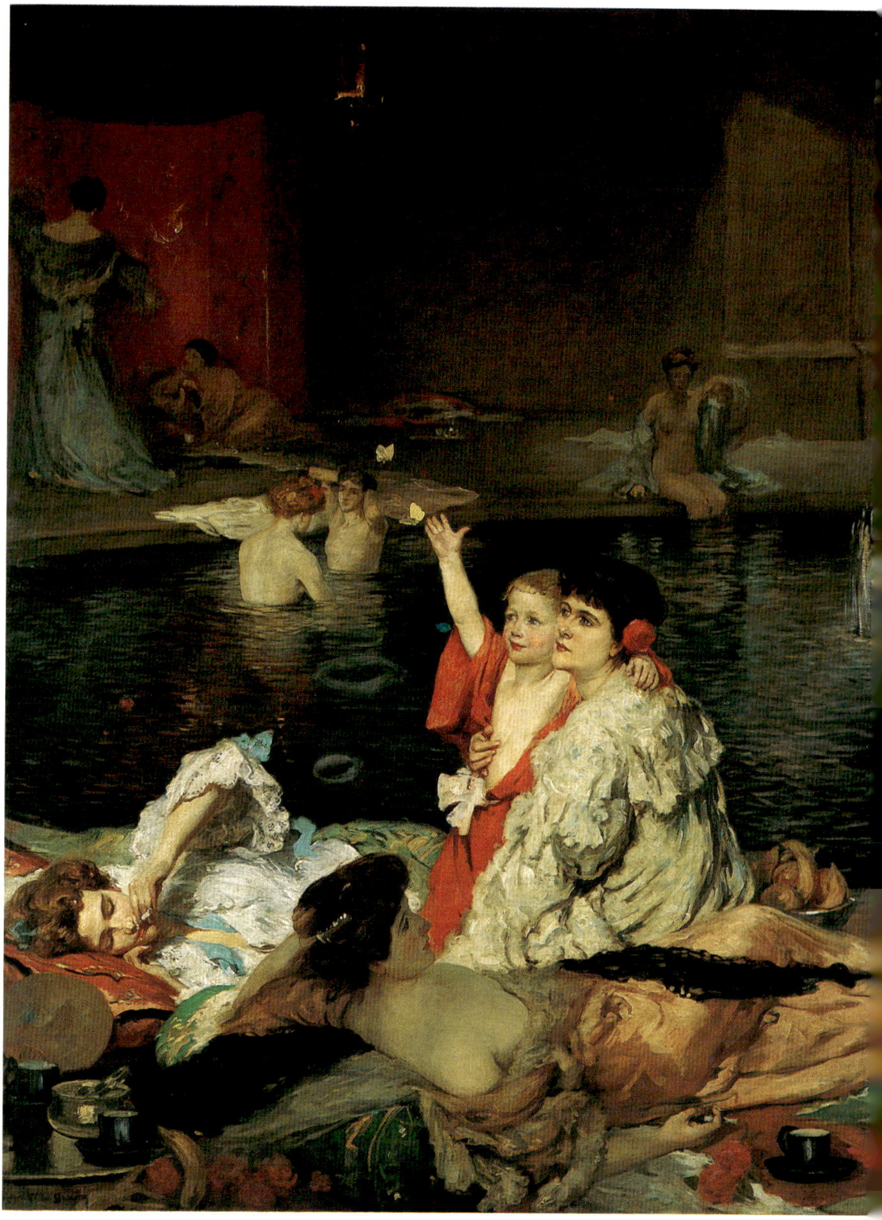

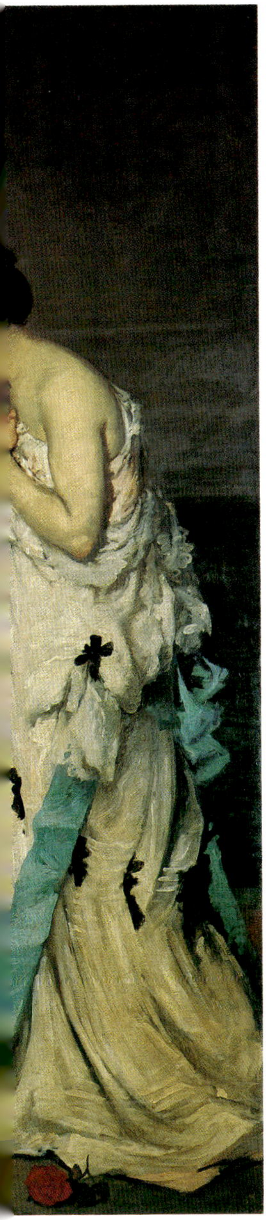

Rupert Bunny
Australia/France 1864–1947
Bathers 1906
Oil on canvas
229.2 x 250cm
Purchased 1988

Rupert Bunny was the first Australian-born artist to achieve a significant reputation both in his own country and overseas. He studied in the 1880s at the National Gallery School, Melbourne with Arthur Streeton and Frederick McCubbin. However, most of his working life—from 1886 to 1932—was spent in France. Bathers *was painted by Bunny in 1906 and exhibited that year in the New Salon, Paris. Appropriately sumptuous in scale, composition and quality of painting,* Bathers *celebrates (and overstates) the luxurious possibilities of Edwardian life.*

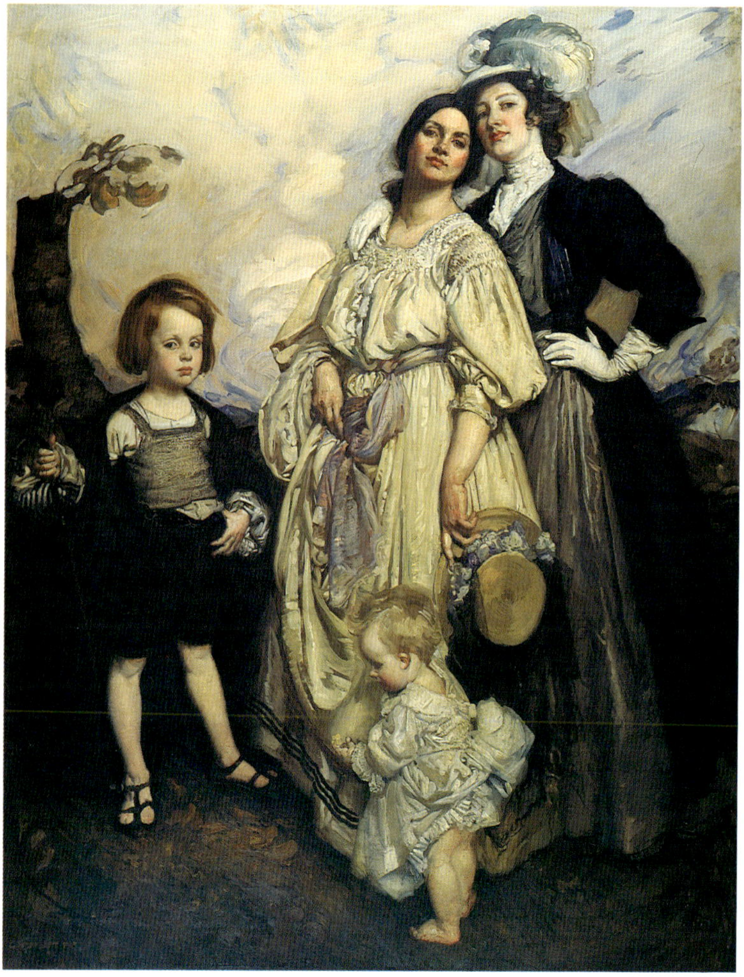

George W. Lambert
Australia NSW 1873–1930
The mother 1907
Oil on canvas
204.6 x 162.5cm
Purchased with the assistance of S.H. Ervin 1965

In this work the artist's wife, Amy, and artist Thea Proctor (Lambert's model, pupil and colleague) stand together in an almost confronting pose, quite separate from the two Lambert children, Maurice and Constant. Lambert's interest in the grand tradition of portraiture can be seen in his bold composition and the emphasis on costume. The vigorous handling of texture and colour reveals the influences of Velasquez, Gainsborough and Van Dyck.

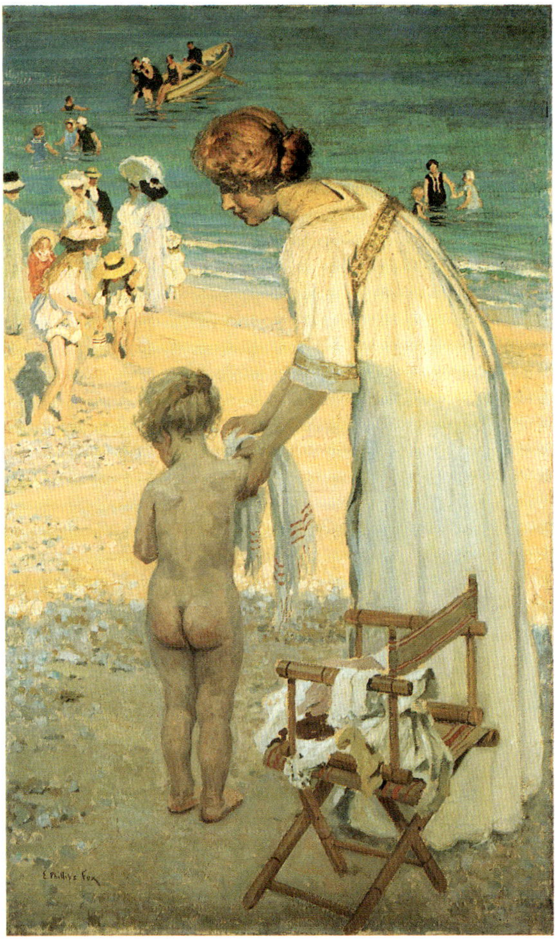

E. Phillips Fox
Australia/France 1865–1915
Bathing hour
(L'Heure de bain) c.1909
Oil on canvas
183.5 x 113.5cm
Purchased 1946

Phillips Fox trained at the National Gallery School, Melbourne and spent much of his career in France and England, gradually absorbing the influences of an impressionism much modified by its later practitioners. Bathing hour, *which was exhibited at the Royal Academy, London in 1910 and the Paris Salon in 1912, typifies the subject matter for which he is most renowned: light-filled images of middle-class women (and sometimes children) at leisure.*

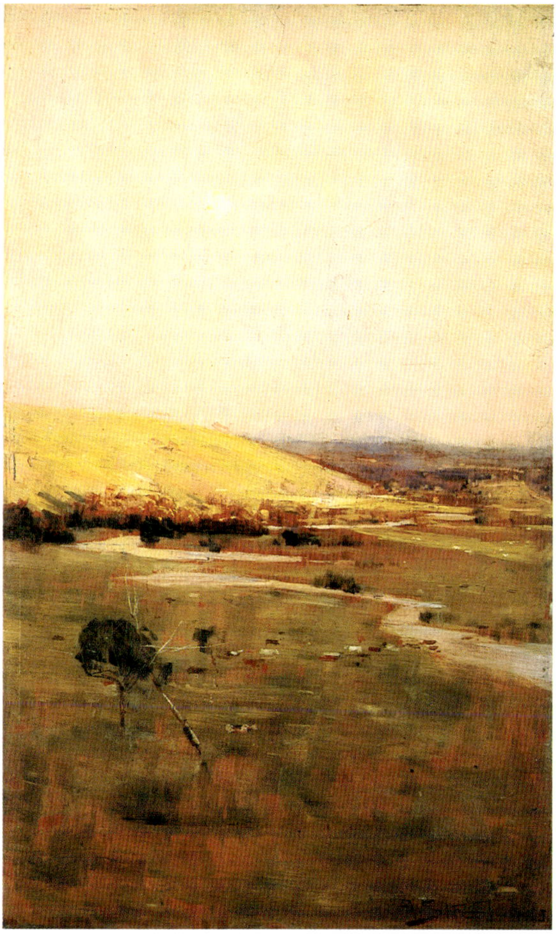

Above
Arthur Streeton
Australia NSW 1867–1943
Sketch for 'Still glides the stream and shall forever glide' 1895
Oil on cedar panel
42 x 26.5cm
Gift of Lady Trout 1978

This work is believed to be a study for the major oil painting of the same name, now in the Art Gallery of New South Wales. The 'stream' is the Yarra River near Heidelberg, then a bush suburb of Melbourne popular with day-trippers and artists. The painting's modest format and gentle tones are typical of the spontaneous, natural effects sought by artists of the Heidelberg School.

Below
Walter Withers
Australia Vic. 1854–1914
Wet day c.1892
Oil on board
25.5 x 32.6cm
Purchased 1982 with funds from Jack, David and Melissa Manton through the Queensland Art Gallery Foundation

Born in England in 1854, Walter Withers arrived in Melbourne in 1882, at the age of twenty-eight. His first eighteen months in Australia were spent working in the bush. A committed pleinairist, Withers became a well-known member of the circle now known as the Heidelberg School, though his landscape style tended to be softer and more atmospheric than that of many of his contemporaries. Wet day *is a small genre painting which is related to the urban landscapes of Streeton during the 1880s.*

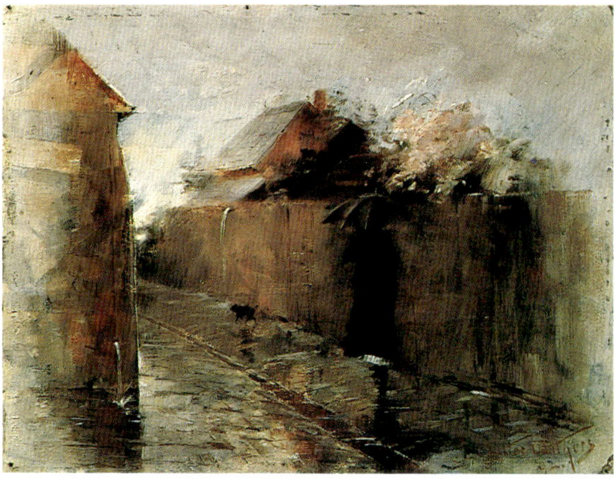

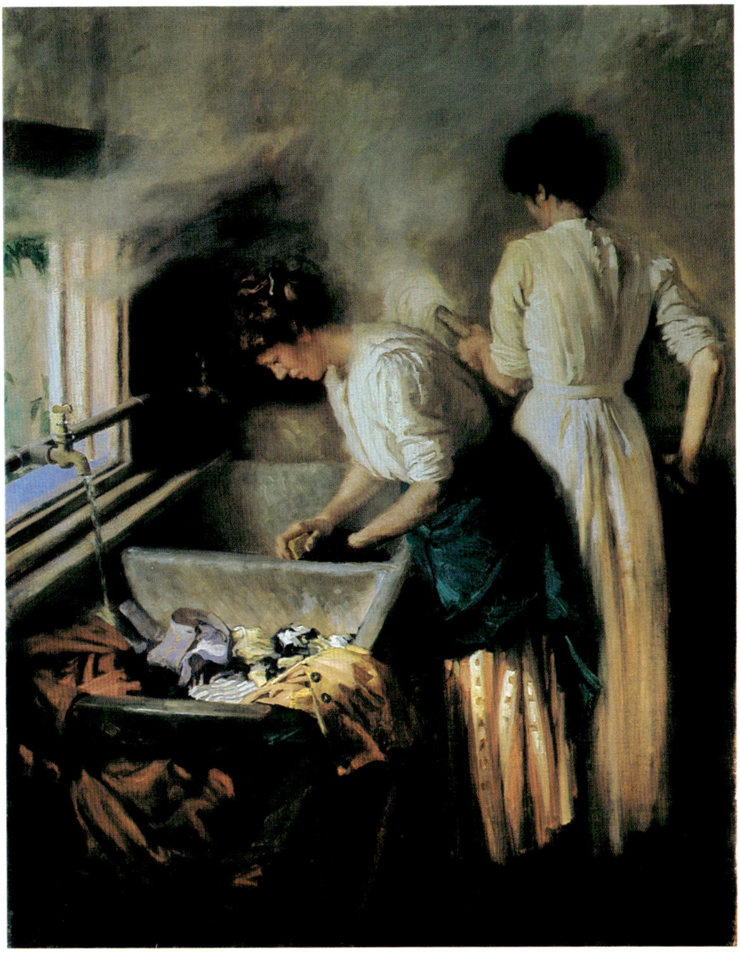

Vida Lahey
Australia Qld 1882–1968
Monday morning 1912
Oil on canvas
153 x 122.7cm
Gift of Madame Emily Coungeau through the Queensland Art Society 1912

Monday morning *is the painting which heralded the beginning of Vida Lahey's serious career. The artist completed this work three years after her return from the National Gallery School, Melbourne, and the style and composition of* Monday morning *are typical of the large-scale genre paintings favoured by her teachers. The painting pre-dates Lahey's trip to Europe and her absorption of more modernist influences. The scale of the painting elevates but does not sentimentalise the subject—the hardship of domestic labour.*

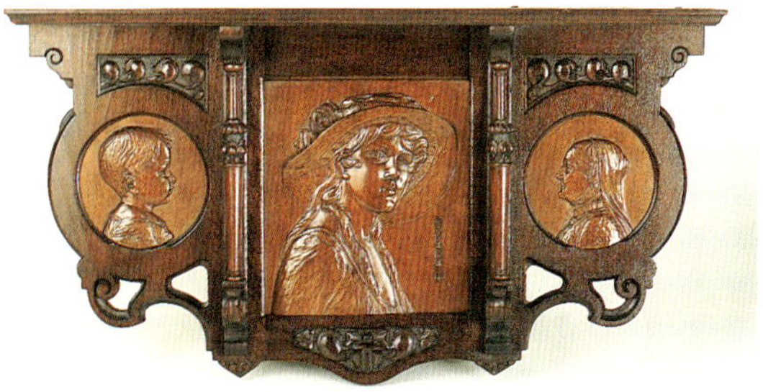

Left
L. J. Harvey
Australia Qld 1871–1949
Wallbracket: Infancy, Youth and Maturity c.1912
Carved beech panels and silky oak
49.5 x 95.2 x 13.3cm
Purchased 1987. Queensland Art Gallery Foundation

L.J. Harvey was Queensland's most active proponent of the Arts and Crafts movement. He was a superior woodcarver and modeller and also taught pottery to generations of Queensland women, founding his own school and a distinctive style. Infancy, Youth and Maturity *was awarded a medal at the British Empire Exhibition in London in 1924. Harvey was particularly fond of studies of the very young or old and such subjects appear constantly in his work.*

Right
Jessie Traill
Australia Vic. 1881–1967
Beautiful victims 1914
Etching
65.4 x 49.3cm (comp.)
Purchased 1961

Beautiful victims, *depicting two men ring-barking a group of stately gums, is the largest etching produced by Traill. This print is both a poignant expression of the artist's concern for the environment and a highly successful exercise in decoration—the flat frieze-like treatment and elements from nature are reminiscent of the art nouveau style.*

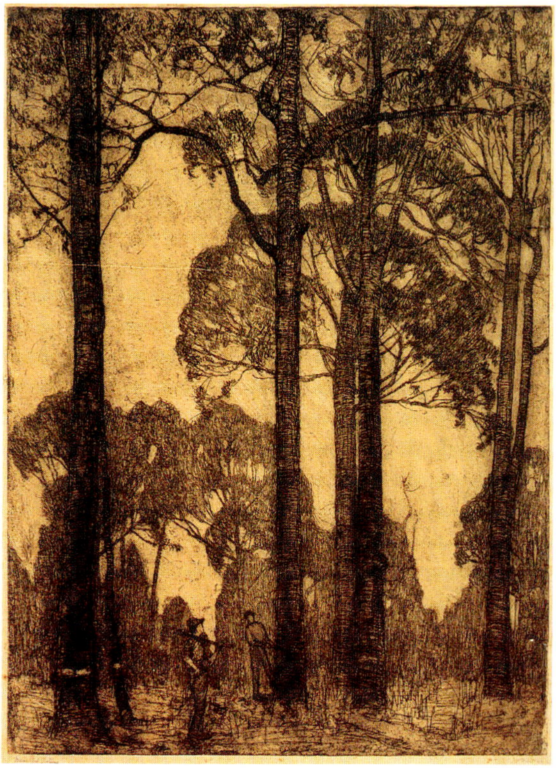

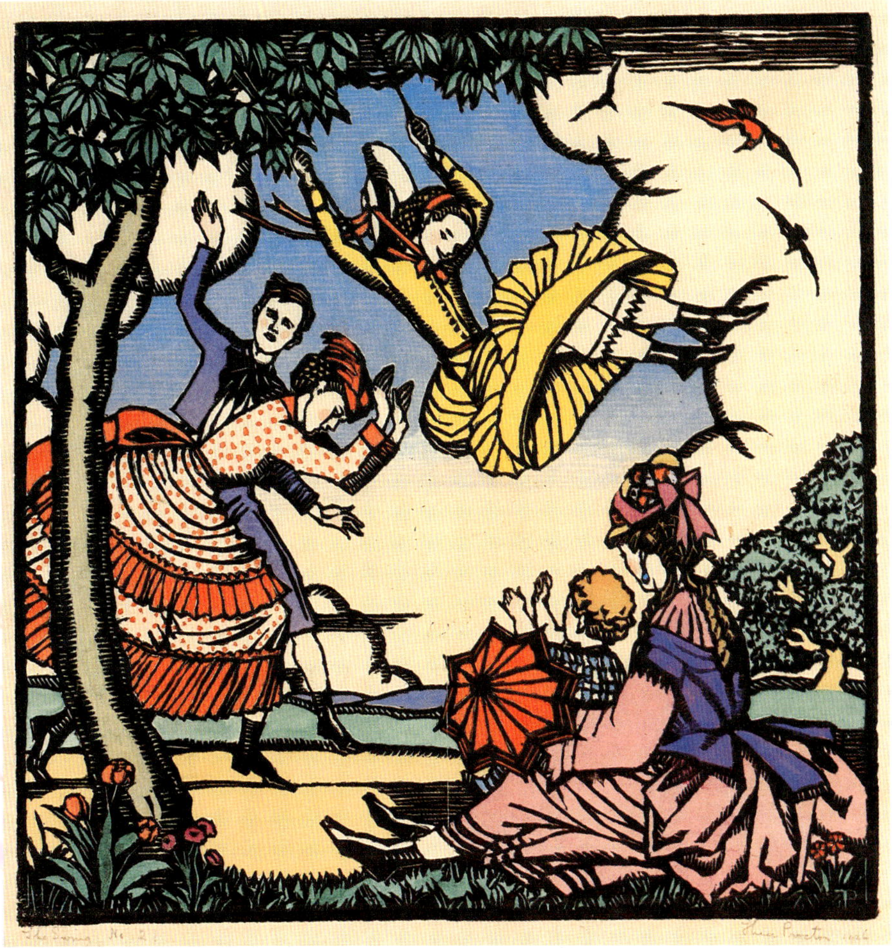

Thea Proctor
Australia NSW 1879–1966
The swing 1925
(printed 1926)
Hand-coloured woodcut
25.1 x 24.9cm (comp.)
Purchased 1980

Thea Proctor was an influential teacher and tastemaker in Sydney during the 1920s and 1930s. She taught design class at Julian Ashton's school and produced sophisticated cover designs for The Home *magazine run by Sydney Ure Smith.* The swing *gives an idea of the decorative stylishness promoted by that publication. Through her teaching of woodcut and linocut, Proctor also brought public attention to these graphic media.*
The artist's first woodcuts were made in 1925 on blocks given to her by Margaret Preston and were intended for children's nursery decorations.

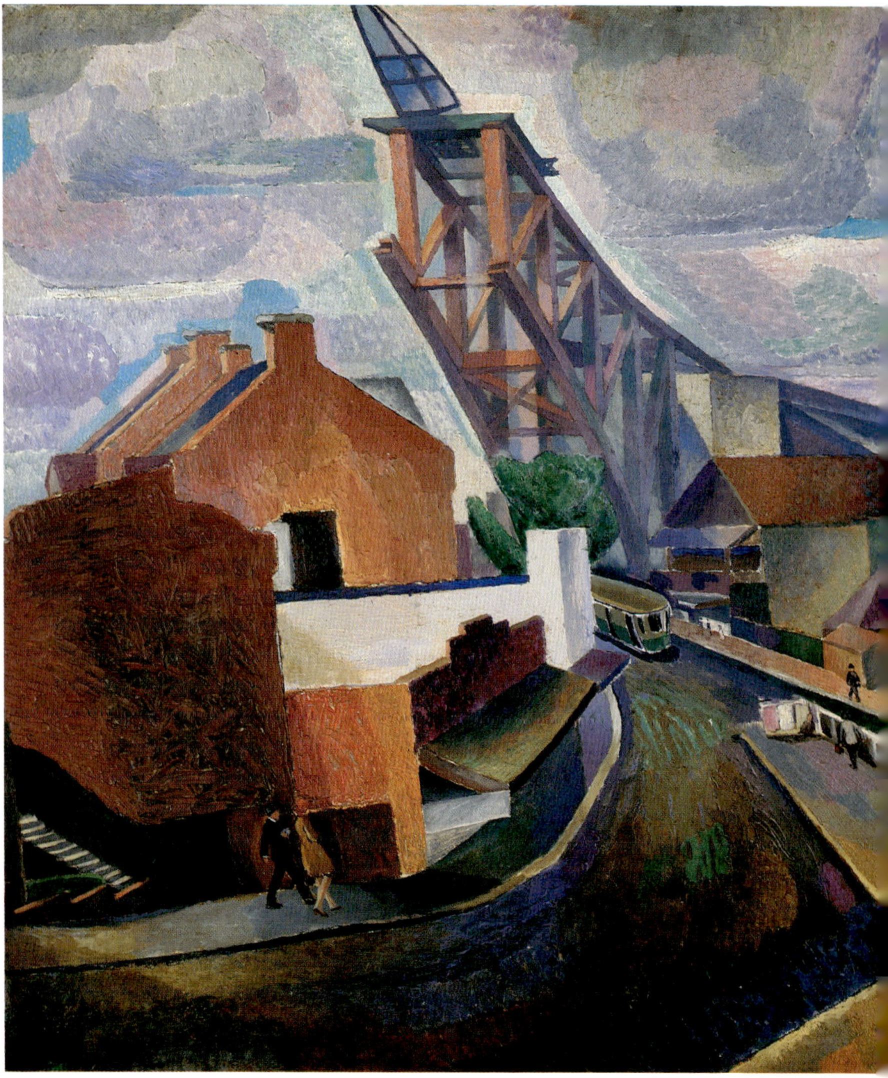

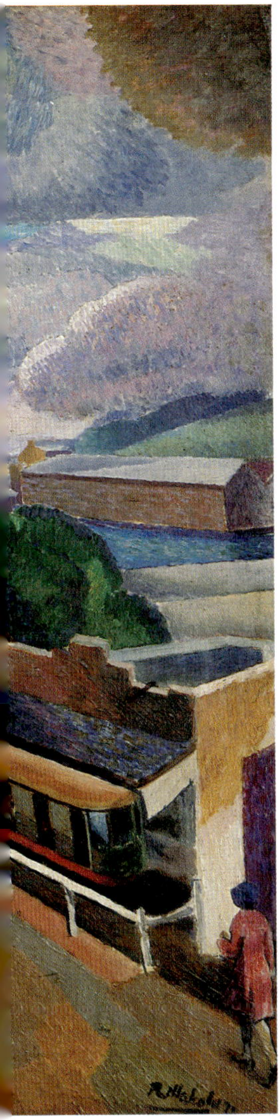

Roland Wakelin
New Zealand/Australia
1887–1971
The Bridge under construction 1928
Oil on composition board
96.5 x 118cm
Purchased 1994. Queensland Art Gallery Foundation Grant. Celebrating the Queensland Art Gallery Centenary 1895–1995

This view of the Sydney Harbour Bridge was painted by Wakelin during its construction in 1928. Influenced by Cézanne and the English vorticists, the artist has made effective use of both colour and form to give the viewer the feeling of being 'pulled' down the slope. Blocks of colour build monumentally to the curve of the arch and then fall away to the buildings on the left in a 'rhythmic flow of line'. The Bridge became a symbol of modernity for artists in the 1920s and 1930s.

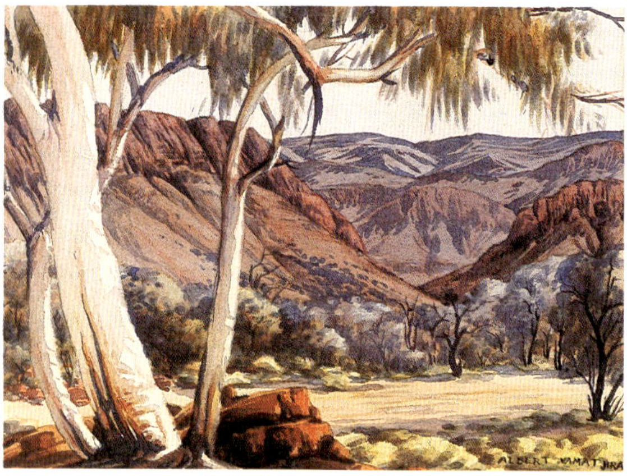

Left
Albert Namatjira
Australia NT 1902–59
Fenns Gap, MacDonnell Ranges c.1936–47
Watercolour over pencil
26.7 x 36.9cm (comp.)
Bequest of George Cedric Tremayne Powne 1979
Reproduced courtesy Legend Press, Sydney

Albert Namatjira was an Aboriginal artist who achieved notable success in the middle decades of the twentieth century. Initially regarded as 'tourist art', Namatjira's watercolours captured the extraordinary colours of the MacDonnell Ranges and became established as popular cultural icons of Australia. Namatjira was clearly influenced by his teacher Rex Battarbee and the Australian watercolourist tradition, but many of his paintings are now also regarded as statements of his Aboriginality and devotion to his land. They detail and inscribe the sacred nature of specific sites and are seen as forerunners of the contemporary Aboriginal art movement.

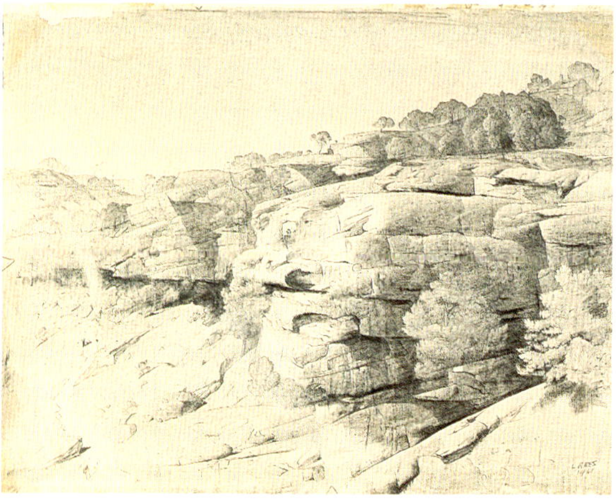

Above
Lloyd Rees
Australia NSW 1895–1988
Sandstone cliffs 1941
Pencil
21.4 x 27.7cm
Purchased 1941

For Lloyd Rees, drawing was essential. His talent was developed through study at the Brisbane Central Technical College, and in 1917 he was invited to move to Sydney and join Smith and Julius, Sydney's foremost commercial art studio at the time. His intensely detailed pencil drawings, especially those of the headlands near his north Sydney home, are considered some of his most important works.

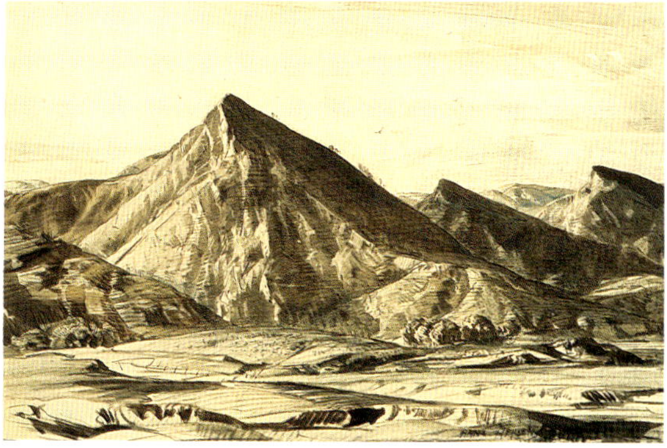

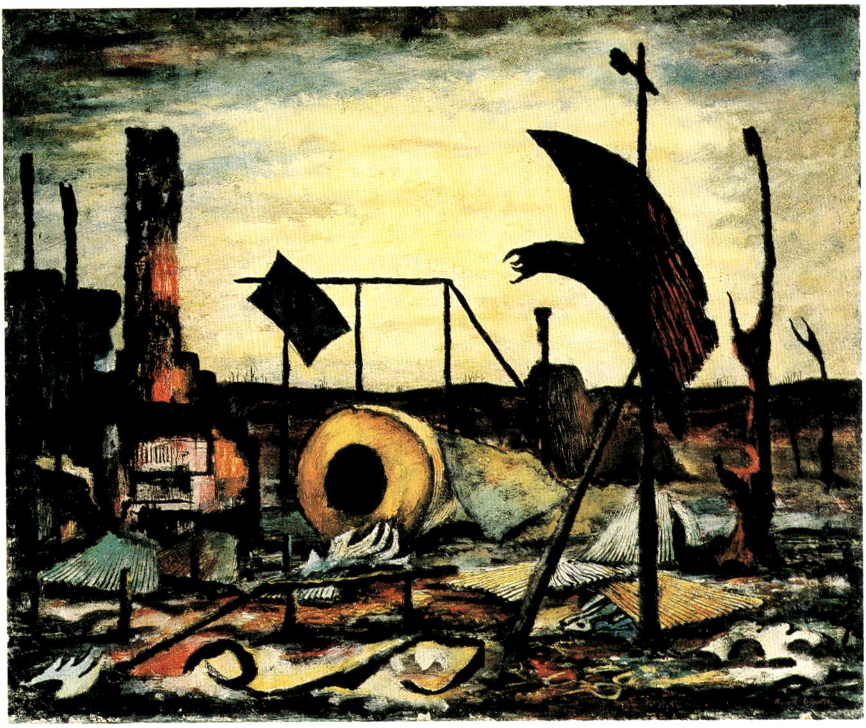

Opposite
Hans Heysen
Australia SA 1877–1968
Three Sisters of Aroona, sunrise 1933
Watercolour over pencil on laid paper on cardboard
29.6 x 40.6cm
Gift of the Godfrey Rivers Trust 1937

Hans Heysen came to Australia from Germany in 1883. He studied art in Adelaide and Paris and, from the time of his first Australian exhibition in 1908, his works were popular examples of Australian landscape art. Heysen worked mainly in South Australia, frequently in the Flinders Ranges, and his watercolour depictions of the bush and surrounding hills won the Wynne Prize for landscape nine times between 1904 and 1932. Heysen's paintings were influential precursors to later watercolourists such as Rex Battarbee and Albert Namatjira.

Above
Russell Drysdale
Australia NSW 1912–81
Bush fire 1944
Oil and ink on canvas on board
62 x 77cm
Gift of Capt. Neil McEacharn through C.L. Harden 1954

Russell Drysdale's landscapes are often animated by traces of human occupation. In Bush fire, the burnt-out remains of a modest farmhouse have become a temporary monument to human fortitude in the face of natural threat. During the 1940s the artist painted a series of images which depict the difficulties of rural life. Drysdale's work, nevertheless, conforms to urban ideas about the harsh interior. The ravaged landscape, painted during the war years, is also symbolic of the economic and military disasters engulfing the world at that time.

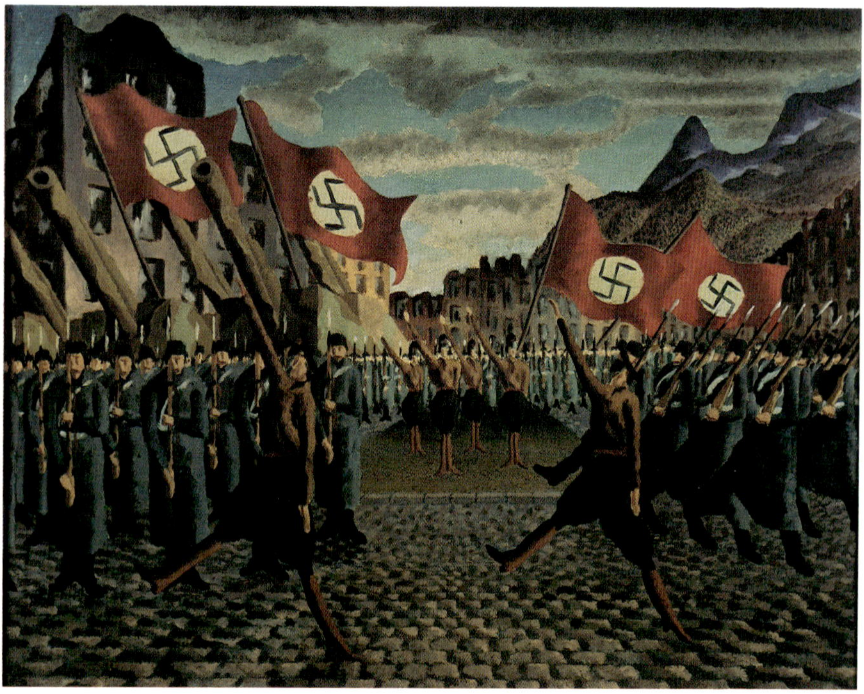

Peter Purves Smith
Australia Vic. 1912–49
The Nazis, Nuremberg
1938
Oil on canvas
71.4 x 91.4cm
Purchased 1961

On 12 March 1938 German troops invaded Austria, which Hitler henceforth declared a province of the German Reich. This painting represents Purves Smith's angry response to this news and to the Nazi rally held in Nuremberg at that time. He depicts the soldiers as faceless, goose-stepping elements of the Nazi war machine. Their backdrop of destruction is a reminder of the devastation caused by war in the past, and a warning of what might come. Similarly, cartoons of the period often commented on the mindless, military mentality of the Nazis.

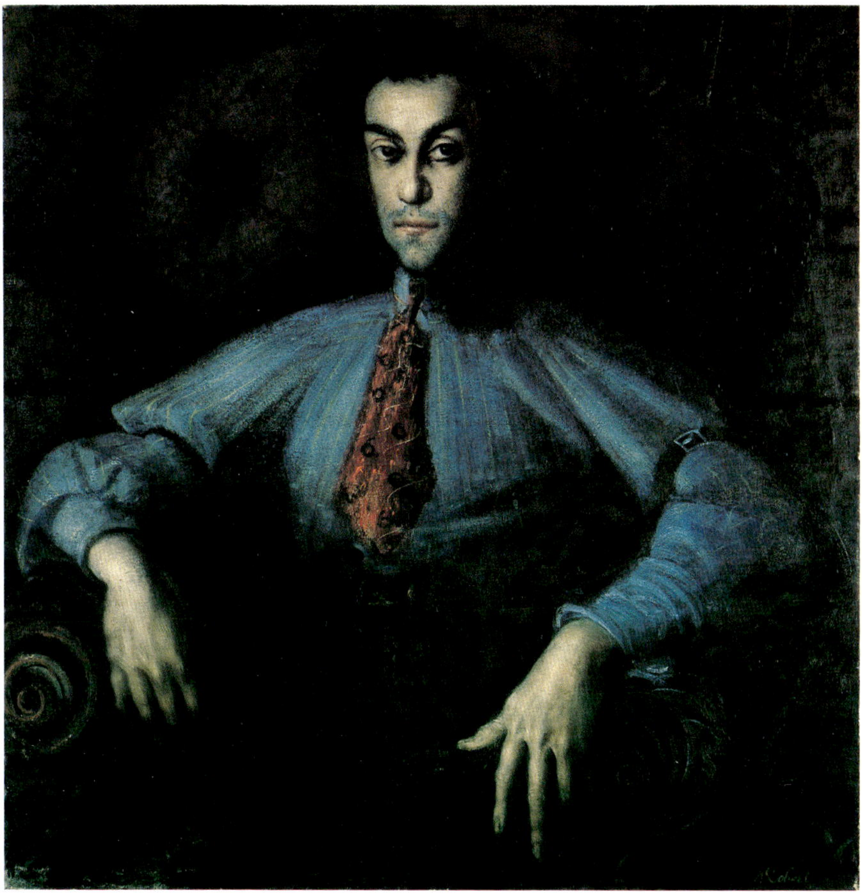

William Dobell
Australia NSW 1899–1970
The Cypriot 1940
Oil on canvas
123.3 x 123.3cm
Gift of the Godfrey Rivers Trust through Miss Daphne Mayo 1943

The Cypriot *has long been recognised as one of Dobell's key works. The model for this work, and for several others which Dobell produced in a series from 1936, was a Greek Cypriot named Aegus Gabriell Ides, a waiter in a London restaurant frequented by the artist during his extended stay in England before the Second World War.* The Cypriot *is a very considered work which seems to quote the tension and distortion of sixteenth-century mannerist portraiture.*

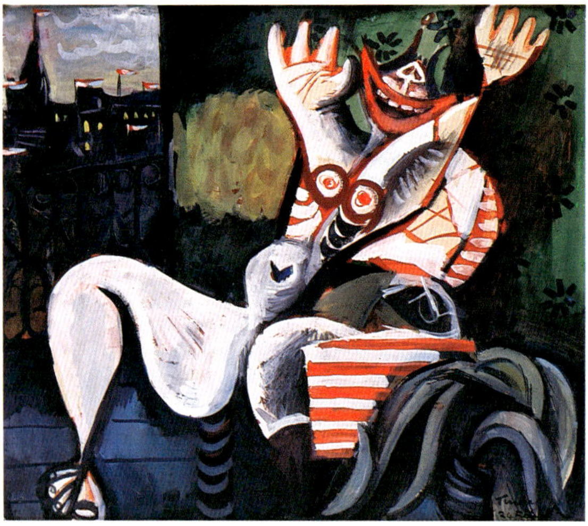

Left
Albert Tucker
Australia Vic. b.1914
Study for 'Images of modern evil: Spring in Fitzroy' 1943
Gouache on paper on board
41 x 47.9cm
Purchased 1995 with a special allocation from the Queensland Government. Celebrating the Queensland Art Gallery Centenary 1895–1995

Tucker's series 'Images of modern evil' dealt with what he saw as the moral decline which accompanied the Second World War. His depiction of the public/private nocturnal world of the inner city is grotesque and dramatic. In this painting the artist projects his sense of revulsion onto the female figures. The influx of American troops during these years contributed to a tense social situation and Tucker's use of fragments of the American flag in this and other paintings is a direct reference to this.

Right
Max Dupain
Australia NSW 1911–92
Meat queue 1946
Gelatin silver photograph
34.2 x 49.5cm
Purchased 1990

Max Dupain began his career in the pictorialist manner, but by 1935 he was recognised as the leading modernist photographer in Australia. During the Second World War he worked as a photographer in the camouflage unit of the RAAF before transferring to the Department of Information in 1945, to take promotional photographs of Australia. At this time Dupain was influenced by documentary film-making with its concern for factual and informative observations of the real world. Meat queue is an example of his work which documents the effects of rationing in post-war Australia.

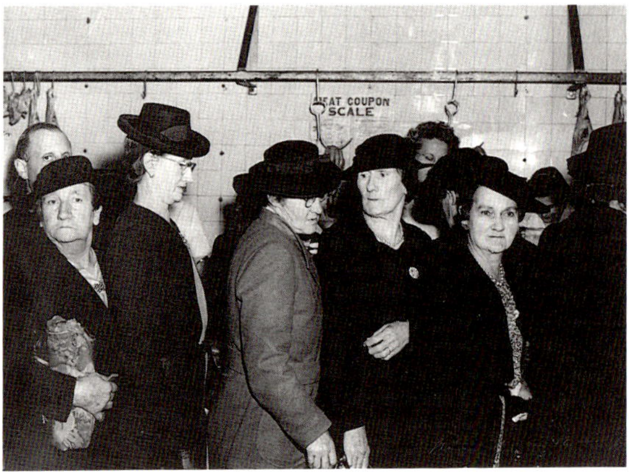

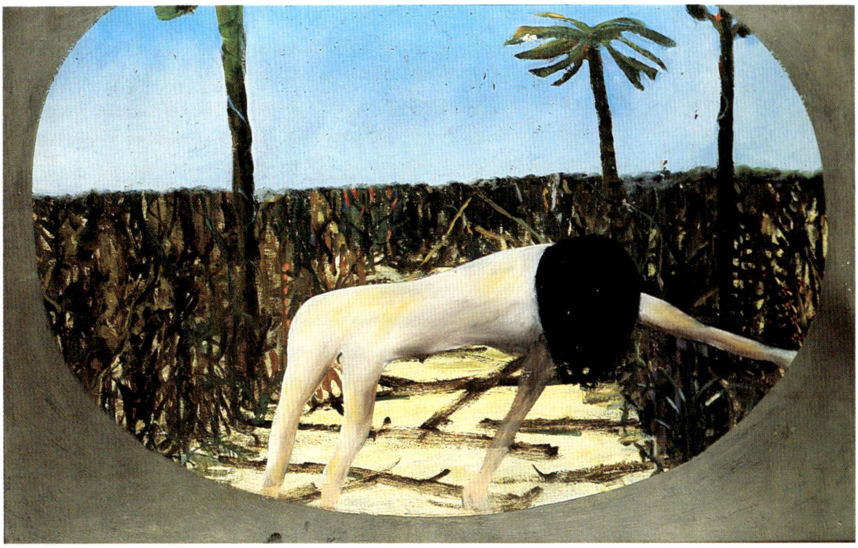

Sidney Nolan
Australia/England 1917–92
Mrs Fraser 1947
Ripolin enamel on hardboard
66.2 x 107 cm
Purchased 1995 with a special allocation from the Queensland Government. Celebrating the Queensland Art Gallery Centenary 1895–1995

When Sidney Nolan visited Brisbane in 1947, the story of Mrs Fraser's shipwreck in the Stirling Castle in 1836 inspired his visit to Fraser Island. Mrs Fraser*, one of his most disturbing works, is one of twelve paintings on this theme which he exhibited at the Moreton Galleries, Brisbane the following year. The artist focuses attention on Mrs Fraser as abject victim. The outsider in an alien environment is a recurrent theme of his work of the 1940s.*

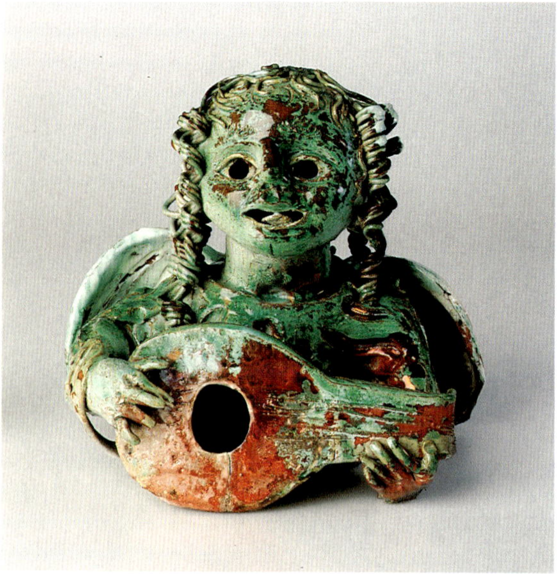

Left
John Perceval
Australia Vic. b.1923
The Herald Angel 1958
Stoneware with reduced copper glazes
26 x 32 x 22cm
Purchased 1960 by public subscription and with the assistance of the Queensland Art Gallery Society

Perceval trained as a painter but was introduced to ceramics through his friend Arthur Boyd and his Murrumbeena pottery. Perceval's figurative decoration for the pottery's service ware was both colourful and vital. He produced a series of whimsical modelled figures of acrobats and angels during the 1950s, of which The Herald Angel *is typical, and which were quite distinctive through his use of reduced copper glazes. Subsequently, he concentrated on painting.*

Right
Daphne Mayo
Australia Qld 1895–1982
The Olympian c.1946
(cast after 1958)
Bronze
94.5 x 31.5 x 23cm
Purchased 1979
Reproduced courtesy Surf Life Saving Queensland Inc. and The Uniting Church in Australia, Queensland Synod

Queensland sculptor Daphne Mayo gained enormous publicity in the late 1920s with her large sandstone pediment carved in situ *for the Brisbane City Hall.* The Olympian's *simplified classical form and full volumes show the influence of French sculptors Rodin and Maillol whose works she undoubtedly saw when she toured France in 1925 and 1938. Daphne Mayo believed in making art publicly accessible and was a strong presence in Queensland art until her death in 1982.*

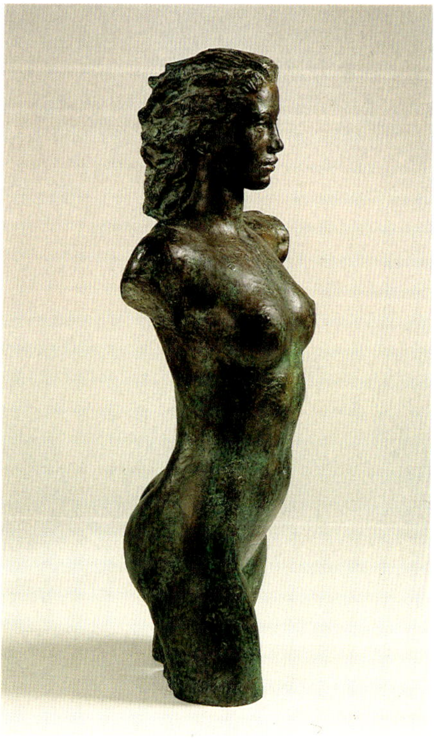

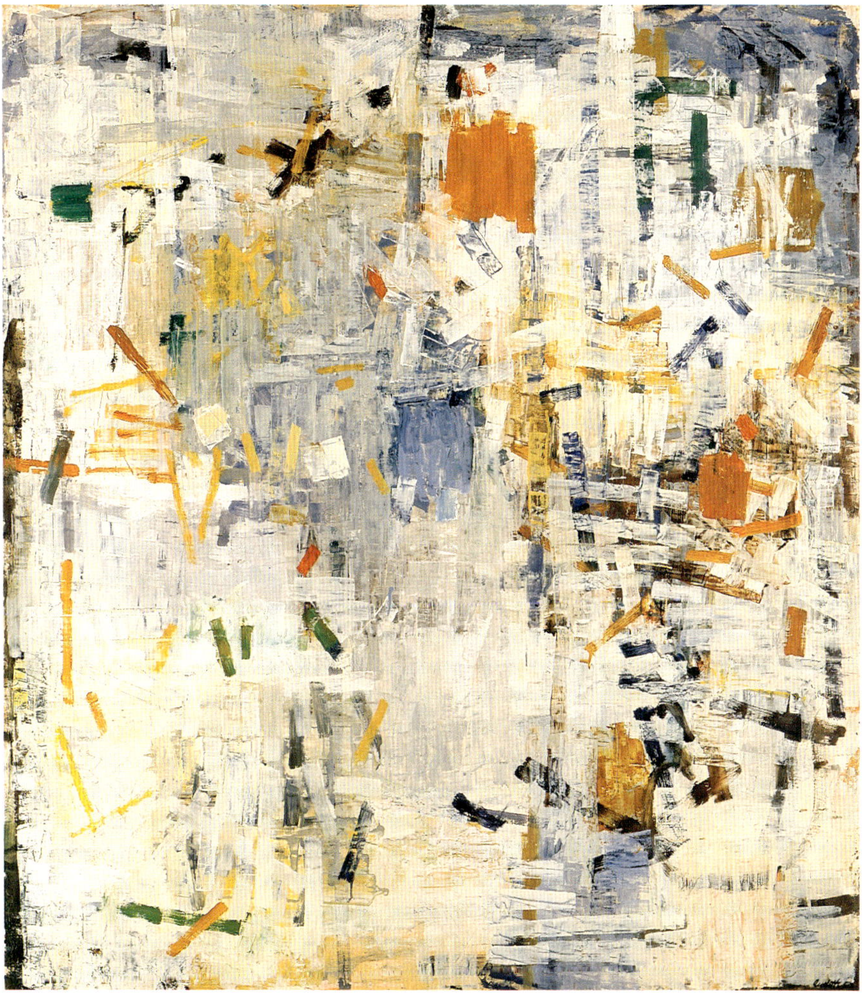

Yvonne Audette
Australia Vic. b.1930
Allegro Serata 1957
Oil on board
122 x 110cm
Purchased 1994.
Godfrey Rivers Trust

Yvonne Audette left Australia in 1952, travelling to New York and Europe. In New York, she spent time with artists Willem de Kooning and Franz Kline and the influence of the abstract expressionists is clear in Allegro Serata. *This painting was inspired by the Romanesque churches around Florence and Milan and its title translates as 'light, happy evening'.*

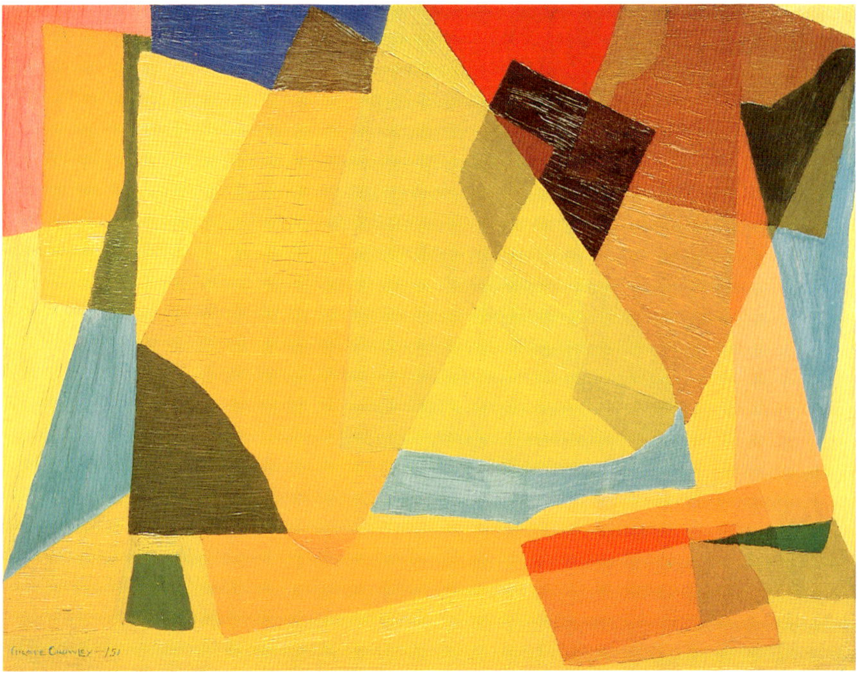

Grace Crowley
Australia NSW 1890–1979
(Abstract) 1951
Oil on cardboard
69 x 91 cm
Purchased 1995. Queensland Art Gallery Foundation

Much of Grace Crowley's life was spent as an influential teacher, which precluded a large personal output. Nevertheless, she was one of the main exponents of modernism in Australia during the 1930s and 1940s. She exhibited her first abstract works (with her colleague Ralph Balson) in 1942. The saturated colours in this painting, influenced by Matisse, construct shapes which overlap, with one colour showing through another like leaves of coloured tissue paper.

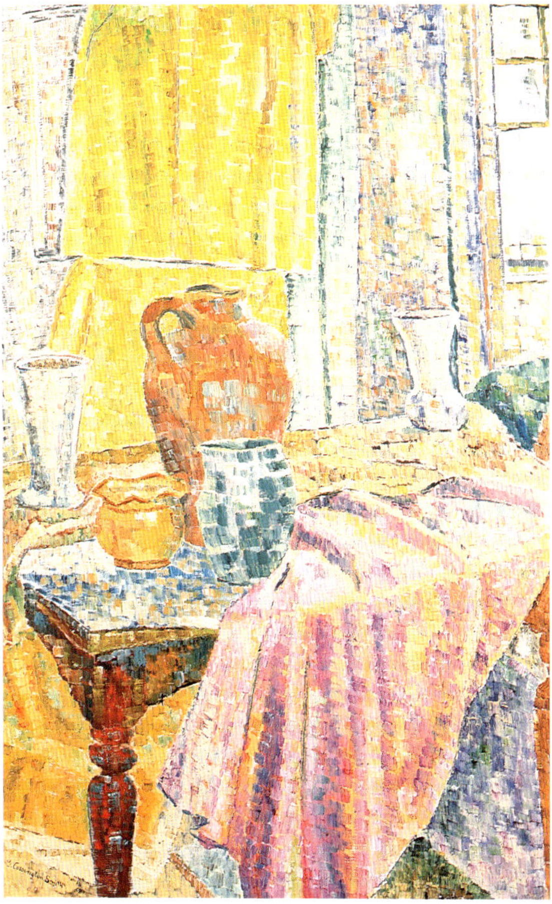

Grace Cossington Smith
Australia NSW 1892–1984
Interior 1958
Oil on composition board
91.4 x 58.1 cm
Gift of the Godfrey Rivers Trust
1958 through Miss Daphne Mayo

Grace Cossington Smith, together with Roland Wakelin and Roy de Maistre, was at the forefront of Australian modernism. She studied in both Australia and Europe and was influenced by post-impressionism, particularly the work of Van Gogh, and later Cézanne and Seurat. The interior of her Turramurra home was the inspiration for many works. Colour was always of primary importance to Grace Cossington Smith and the use of yellow in this work reflects its ability to create light.

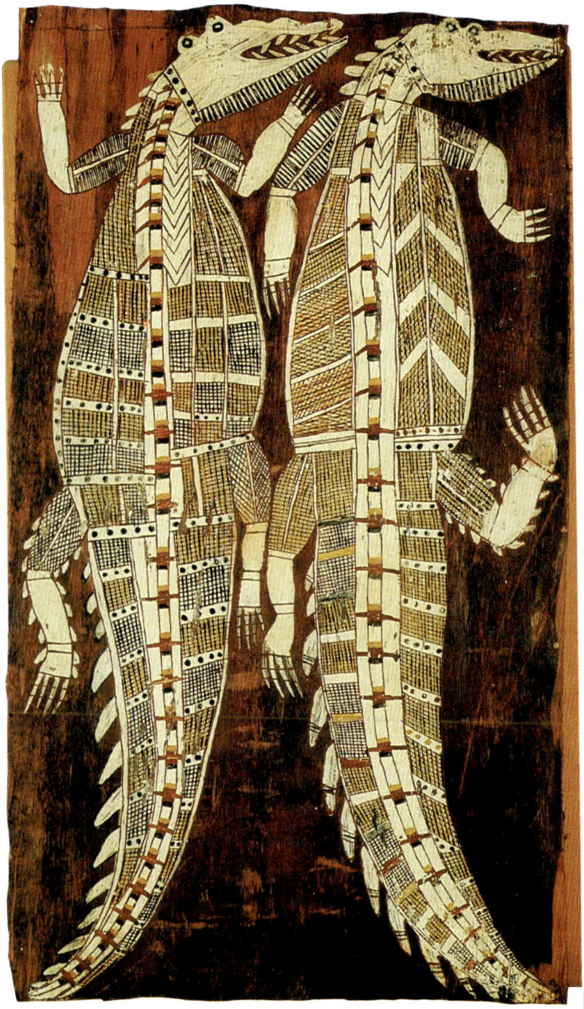

Yirawala
Australia NT 1903–76
Two crocodiles 1958
Natural pigments on bark
105 x 58.5cm
Purchased 1971
Reproduced courtesy
Mrs Sandra LeBrun Holmes, Sydney

Yirawala is one of the best known twentieth-century Aboriginal artists. He produced paintings as a form of instruction, to tell stories which explain the origin and meaning of people, places and animals. The subject matter of his paintings is taken from stories associated with ceremonies and represents the spirits of natural species which occur in the Arnhem Land environment.

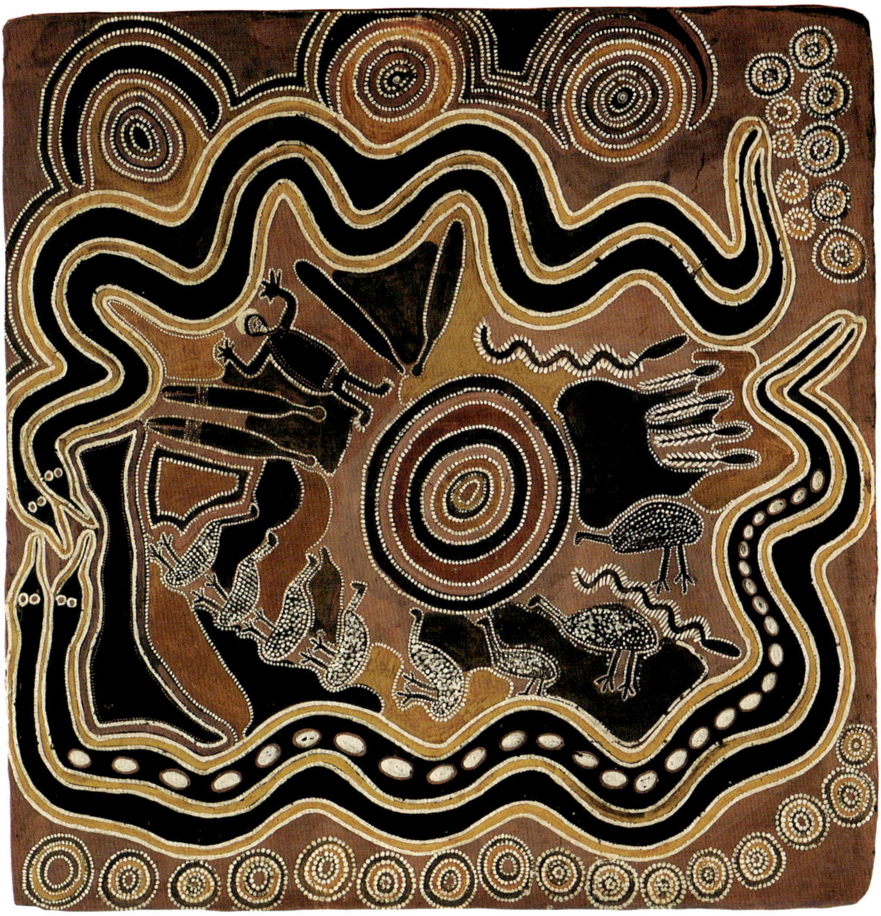

Nym Bunduk
Australia WA c.1907–81
Nakymal painting (Murrinh-Patha totemic landscape) c.1959–60
Oil on board
122 x 122cm
Gift of Mrs Lillian Bosch 1972

This panel by Nym Bunduk is one of three which originally decorated the Port Keats Mission Church in the Northern Territory. It is a free adaptation of the creation myths of the Murinbata people. The other panels are in the collections of the Musée d'Homme, Paris and the Basle Ethnographic Museum.

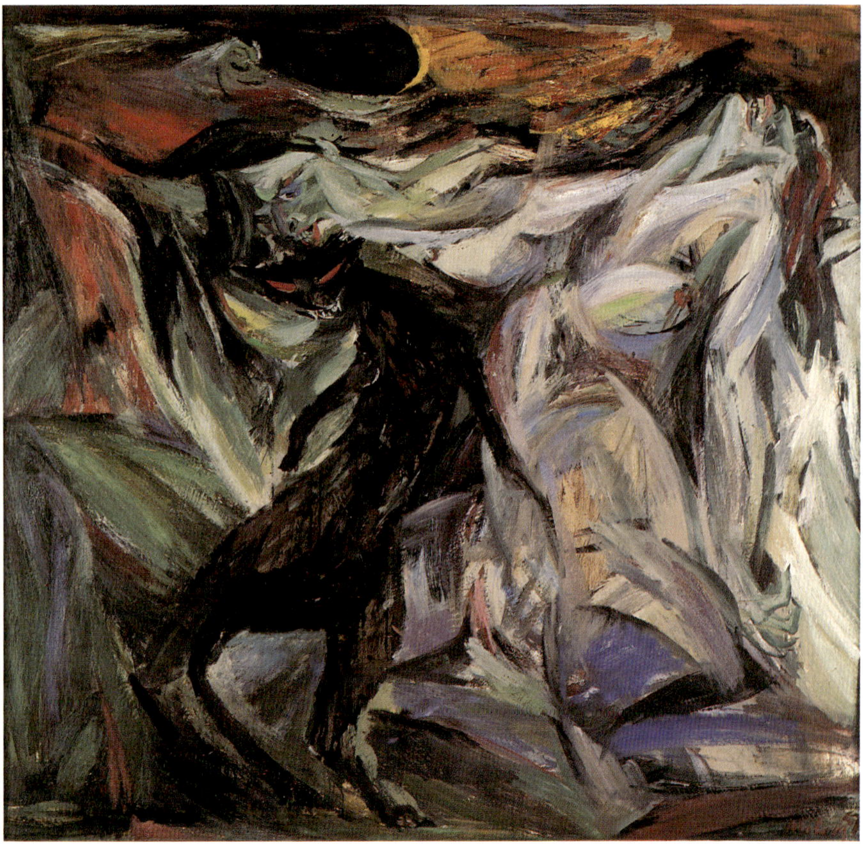

Jon Molvig
Australia Qld 1923–70
A twilight of women 1957
Oil on composition board
137.2 x 148.6cm
Purchased 1984

Jon Molvig was a major influence on the Brisbane art scene. The vigour of his expressive brushwork and almost violent compositional form in A twilight of women *emerged from an intensely creative and productive period of the artist's life in the late 1950s. This and other works from these years established Molvig's reputation as a figurative expressionist.*
The subject of the painting is thematically linked to a series which explored brooding, nocturnal images of lovers, prostitutes and lunatics.

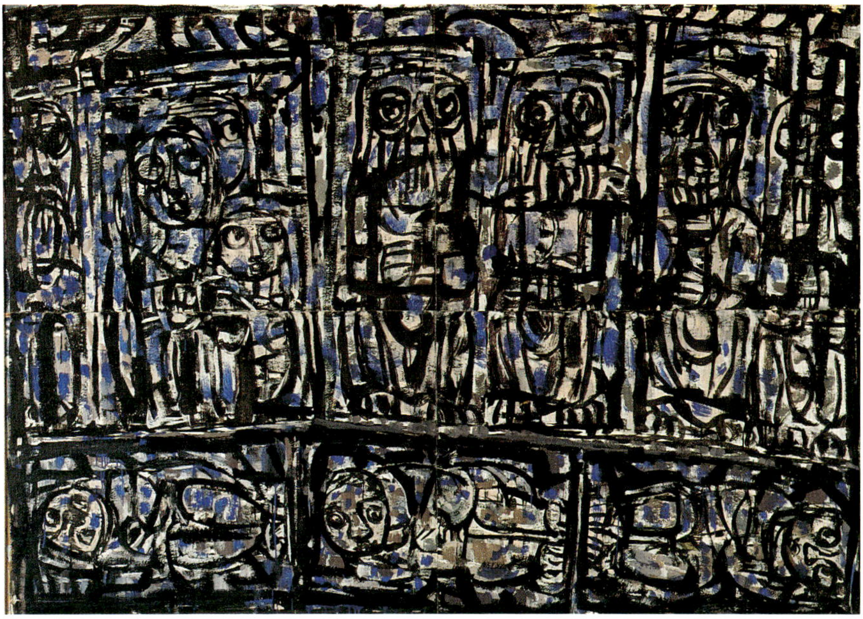

Ian Fairweather
Scotland/Australia 1891–1974
Epiphany 1962
Synthetic polymer paint on cardboard
139.6 x 203.2cm
Purchased 1962

The feast of the Epiphany commemorates the visit of the Wise Men to the infant Jesus. King Herod, on hearing the Magi were honouring the new-born King of the Jews, ordered all male children under two years old to be killed. In a dream, Joseph was warned by an angel to take his family to safety in Egypt. Fairweather's painting shows, from left to right: Herod, the Holy Family, the Three Magi and the innocent children. The use of heavy black line over indigo conveys an impression of stained glass, reminiscent of cathedrals.

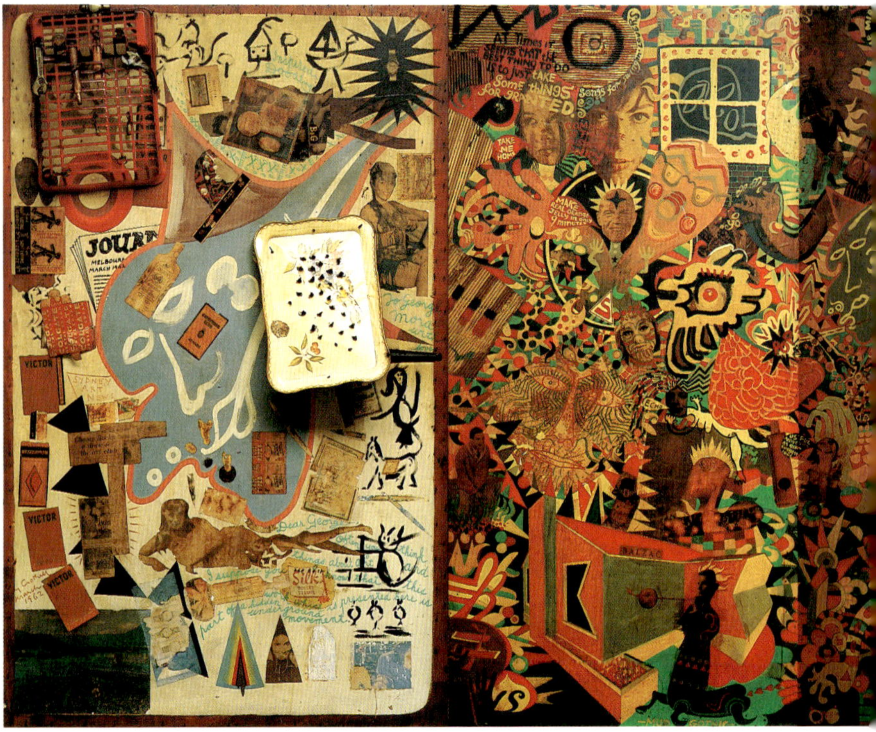
At times it seems that the best thing to do is to just take some things for granted.
Take me home
Make real orange jelly in 9 minutes
JOUR
VICTOR
VICTOR
VICTOR
Dear George

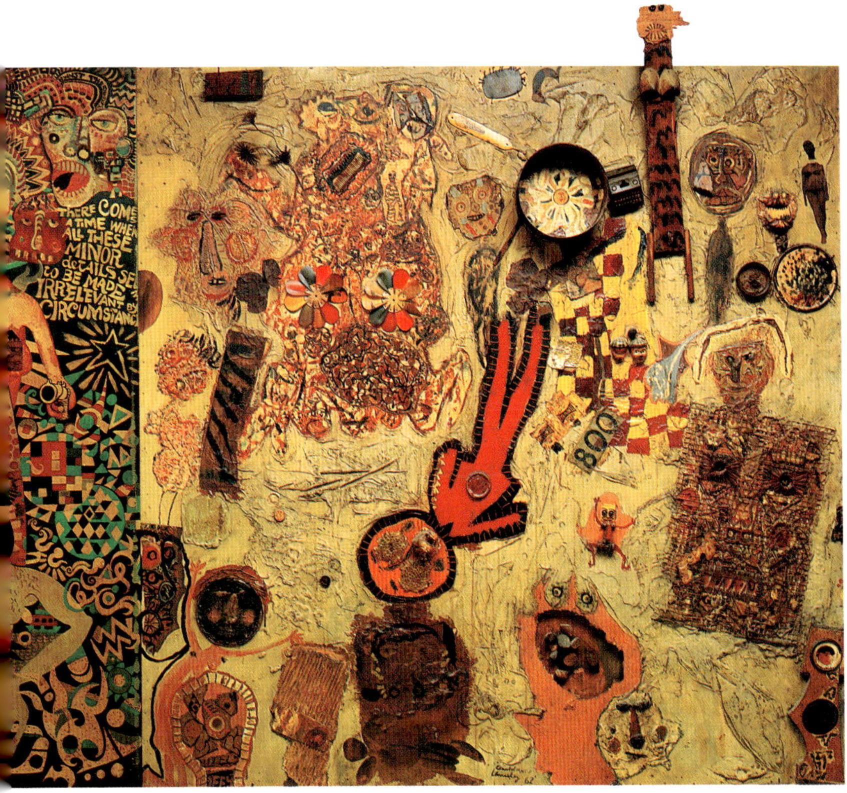

Mike Brown
Australia Vic. b.1938
Ross Crothall
Australia NSW b.1934
Colin Lanceley
Australia NSW b.1938
The Café Balzac mural
1962
Oil, synthetic polymer paint and mixed media collage on plywood panels
Triptych: 195.3 x 487.4cm (overall)
Purchased 1988

This mural was commissioned by Georges Mora from the Annandale Imitation Realists, a group of Sydney artists consisting of Mike Brown, Ross Crothall and Colin Lanceley. The artists each worked on a panel and completed the triptych on site at Mora's Café Balzac, one of the key meeting and eating places of the Melbourne cultural scene in the 1950s. Their work was ironic and irreverent, and functioned as a 'de-bunking' of the calculated preciousness of art objects.

Contemporary Australian Art

Contemporary art is the art of today. Contemporary visual art presents material evidence of the visual, emotional and conceptual dialogue that currently exists between artists and their perceived worlds. The process of making and responding to art offers a vital avenue of discovery and communication, both for the artist who creates the work and for the viewer who engages with it. The desire to impose a singular and static meaning upon the experience of viewing art is constantly being challenged. The dynamic experience and interpretation of a work of art depends on the viewer's own culturally determined perceptions, observations, individual insights, feelings and memories.

The Queensland Art Gallery's contemporary Australian art collection encompasses those works produced since 1965. In the 1960s, abstraction became a prevailing force in Australian art. A more detached, intellectual style was established, dealing with ideas of modernity which contrasted with the more literal narrative of representational art. The abstract austerity of this work contrasts strongly with the expressionism of Jon Molvig and his circle, which prevailed in Queensland at that time. New York rather than Europe was the focus for many Australian artists in the 1960s, while in Australia, Sydney's Central Street Gallery (1966–70) became the centre for new abstract art. The shift in focus was accomplished with two exhibitions, 'Two Decades of American Painting' 1966 and 'The Field' 1968. The latter exhibition of Australian art was selected for the opening of the National Gallery of Victoria at the St Kilda Road site and included the work of David Aspden, Robert Jacks, Alun Leach-Jones, Robert Hunter and Robert Rooney. Rooney's *Kind-hearted kitchen-garden I* 1967 is a work from this period.

The quest to define Australian culture within an international context accompanies much of the art produced in this country. In addition to the indigenous peoples, artists born into cultures other than Anglo-Saxon have made a major contribution to the development of cultural life in Australia since the Second World War. During the past three decades, Australians have developed a much more complex sense of what their international context might be.

In *Portrait of Arthur Rimbaud* 1970–71, Australian-born Brett Whiteley looked to Europe for inspiration and identification, aligning himself with the defiantly rebellious spirit of the nineteenth-century French poet. The compelling and challenging writing in Rimbaud's *A Season in Hell* is the specific reference for this mixed media work, which charts the parallel journeys of hellish self-exploration experienced by both the artist and the poet.

Tympan 1977 is a collaborative work which alludes to architectural and conceptual themes in twelfth and thirteenth-century French cathedrals. This painting is the result of a unique collaboration between five nationally renowned artists: George Baldessin, Roger Kemp, Les Kossatz, Mirka Mora and Andrew Sibley. Within this painted tympan, each artist was then free to express individual visual concerns. Each artist's own belief systems and cultural values were incorporated as the collaboration was negotiated and resolved.

Originally from Chile, Juan Davila is now based in Melbourne. His art is potent and intentionally provocative, confronting ideas of cultural and economic colonialism and the manipulative aspects of consumerism in our media-saturated society. The 'appropriation' or 'quotation' of existing images and ideas has been explored by a number of artists in the past, and has been given particular emphasis in the twentieth century by artists such as Pablo Picasso, Marcel Duchamp and Andy Warhol. During the 1980s, however, appropriation became a dominant feature of international art practice. This concept was employed by artists as they examined and questioned modes of representation and conventions that have become institutionalised through art history and the art market. In *Miss Sigmund* 1981, Davila communicates his ideas through overt quotation of imagery, including globally drawn references to 'bad taste', 'fine art', pornography, psychology, the famous and the obscene.

Based in Australia, Bernhard Sachs is an artist whose imagery parallels the psychoanalytical concerns of artists in Europe. Sachs completed *During philosophy—group portrait with head* 1990 after extensive travel in Europe. His work explores international humanist issues of transience, morality, memory, ideology and history through the visual image.

The echoing of imagery from past generations and distant cultures is also present in Stephen Bowers's lustrous 'funky' ceramic work, *Vase: Chintz* 1990. Ceramic traditions are recalled and combined with distinctly Australian visions of botanical decoration. His work is extravagantly and floridly decorative, an ironic statement about the style and tradition of ceramics.

Certain artists working within any culture will consistently pursue original and singular paths. In Queensland over the past few decades, artists such as Ian Fairweather and Jon Molvig have emphasised vigorous, expressive brushstrokes. *Man climbing over images* 1988 by Gordon Shepherdson and Sam Fullbrook's *Ernestine Hill* 1970 are intimate and highly personal works in this style. Shepherdson focuses his energies on the creation of passionate works of psychological insight. These autobiographical works go beyond the outward appearance of things, to express the private language of the soul and mind. The portrait *Ernestine Hill* identifies the unique characters of two fiercely independent people who contributed much to the cultural life of Australia: Hill through her extensive journalism and travel writing, and Fullbrook through his heartfelt paintings.

During the 1960s a group of artists including Arthur Boyd, John Brack, Sidney Nolan, Charles Blackman, John Perceval and Albert Tucker were prominent in bringing Australian art into the international arena. Many of these artists are still significantly shaping artistic life in this country. In his painting *Bathers and Pulpit Rock* 1984–85, Arthur Boyd continues

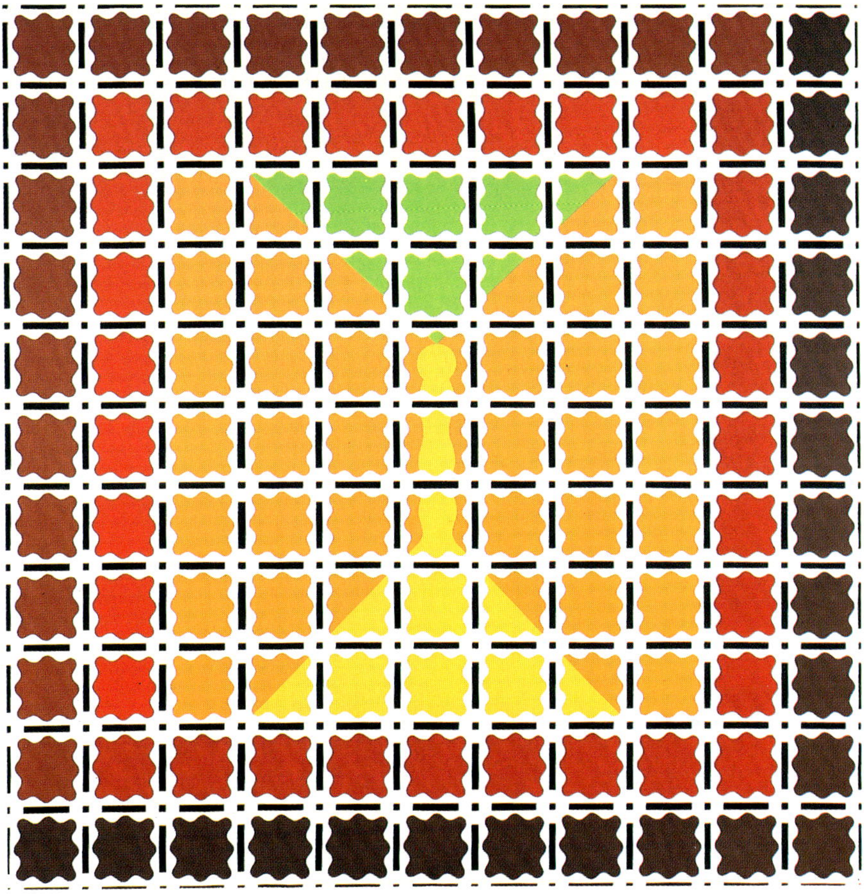

Robert Rooney
Australia Vic. b.1937
Kind-hearted kitchen-garden I 1967
Synthetic polymer paint on canvas
168.3 x 168.3cm
Purchased 1990

Rooney takes commonplace elements from the household environment and incorporates them into grid-like structures that reflect the monotonous pattern of daily life. By his use of the shape of clothes pegs, the scalloped square on a Christmas cake box-top and the title (from a dictionary heading), Rooney acknowledges pop art and its celebration of the banal.

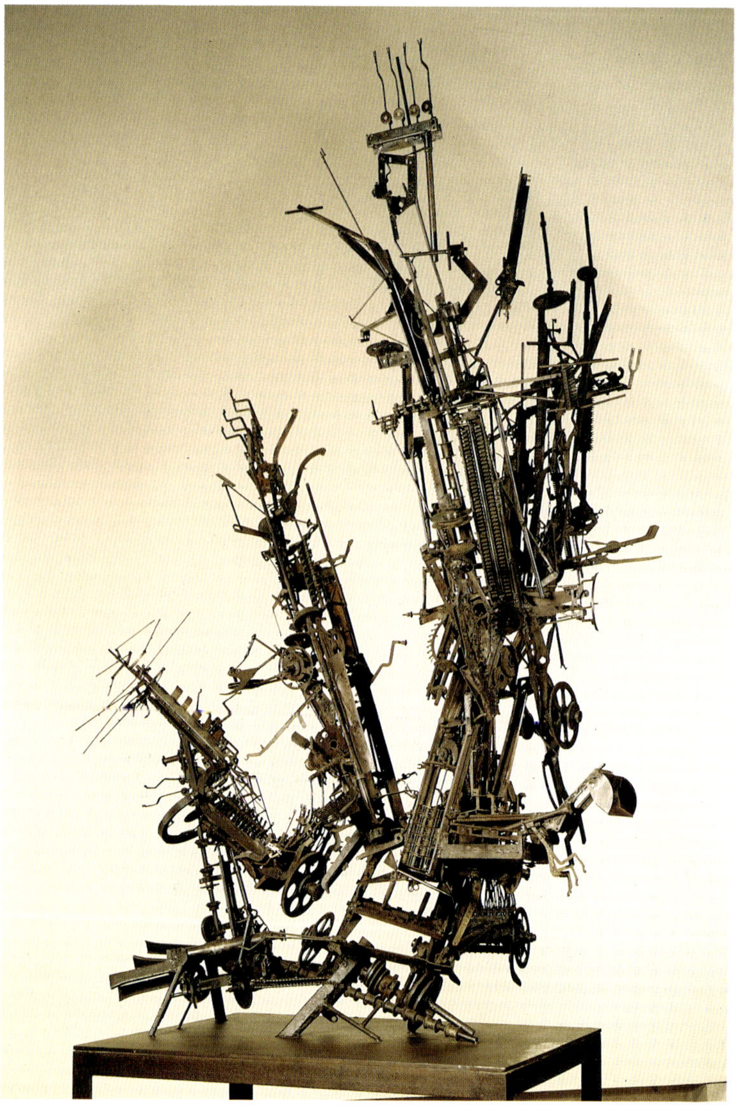

Robert Klippel
Australia NSW b.1920
Opus 247, metal construction 1965–68 1969
Steel and found objects
198 x 145cm x 126cm
(irreg., with base)
Purchased 1983. Queensland
Art Gallery Foundation

Opus 247 can be regarded as the summation of Klippel's experiences during the decade that he spent in the United States (1957–67). The use of 'Opus' in the title has a direct association with musical composition and Klippel has described it as 'a whole exhibition in one work'. Typewriters and other commercial machines are cannibalised to create an organic union of mechanical forms, producing a sculpture which is both taut and elegant.

to explore the theme of dislocated human forces within the harsh antipodean landscape whilst John Brack, in his work *Finale* 1992, continues to use satire to create a threatening conformity in his images.

Fred Williams's visual investigations into the essence of the Australian landscape have quite possibly altered our cultural perception of the land. His work has made an immense contribution to the development of landscape painting in this country. *Yan Yean* 1970 links Williams's earlier Hillside and Hummock series with his final series of Pilbara works.

The paintings of William Delafield Cook interpret the landscape through the visual language of heightened realism, an approach made possible with the technological assistance of photography. Works such as *A haystack* 1982 offer the viewer an intricate and astonishingly detailed representation of what the eye might see.

Another perspective on the landscape is articulated through the delicate brushstrokes and dense surfaces of William Robinson's paintings. These works are not illustrations of the landscape but are about being in a place and having many sensations at once. These works present the landscape experientially, from multiple perspectives. Paintings such as *William and Shirley, flora and fauna* 1985 have captured the imagination of many viewers with their fantastic and almost mythic interpretations of the subtropical Australian rainforest.

William Yaxley, like Robinson, deals with perceptions of the natural world. Both artists imbue their images of nature with engaging humour. *The mangrove monster no. 2* 1986 is fabricated by Yaxley from recycled natural and manufactured materials, and is simultaneously part beast, part foliage, part reptile and part nightmare.

From a more global perspective, issues concerning the world environment and our place within it are addressed by artists such as Bea Maddock. Her photo-etching *Square* 1972 is drawn from a photograph and shows the alienation of the individual within an urban situation.

The intimate relationship between the land and art is intrinsic to the cultural life of traditional Aboriginal peoples. *Bush Grain Dreaming (Watiyawarnu Jukurrpa)* 1990 by Dolly Nampijinpa Daniels is an example of recent visual art from the central Australian desert. In the early 1970s a remarkable development took place in the art of central Australia, as ceremonial body painting and ground designs were adapted to paintings done with European art materials. Small desert communities became important centres of art production for exhibitions and collections which proliferated nationally and internationally. One of these desert communities is Yuendumu, where women are an important force in the new art form and Dolly Nampijinpa Daniels is the most senior and respected female painter. Emily Kame Kngwarreye began painting canvases late in her life and has become one of the most admired Australian artists of the 1990s. Her *Wild Potato Dreaming* 1990 is an especially beautiful example of the way the secrecy surrounding certain themes in Aboriginal art is respected by submerging the precise details of the composition within superimposed layers of dots.

Trevor Nickolls is an urban Aboriginal artist whose work *From Dreamtime 2 Machinetime* 1979 clearly presents the duality confronting the cultural identity of Aborigines in Australia today. He attempts to bridge the gap between Aboriginal and non-Aboriginal art by incorporating both Aboriginal and European techniques.

Ken Thaiday, a Torres Strait Islander, constructs dance masks such as *Shark mask (with bait fish)* 1995. Mask works are a traditional art form of the Torres Strait Islanders; however, Thaiday does not strictly adhere to family or clan tradition as he creates his own designs and utilises a variety of materials.

The recent paintings of Gordon Bennett continue the dialogue between Aboriginal and non-Aboriginal art through the heart, mind and eyes of an urban Aboriginal artist. Bennett's work is informed by post-modern thought concerning the meanings, cultural contexts and symbolism of

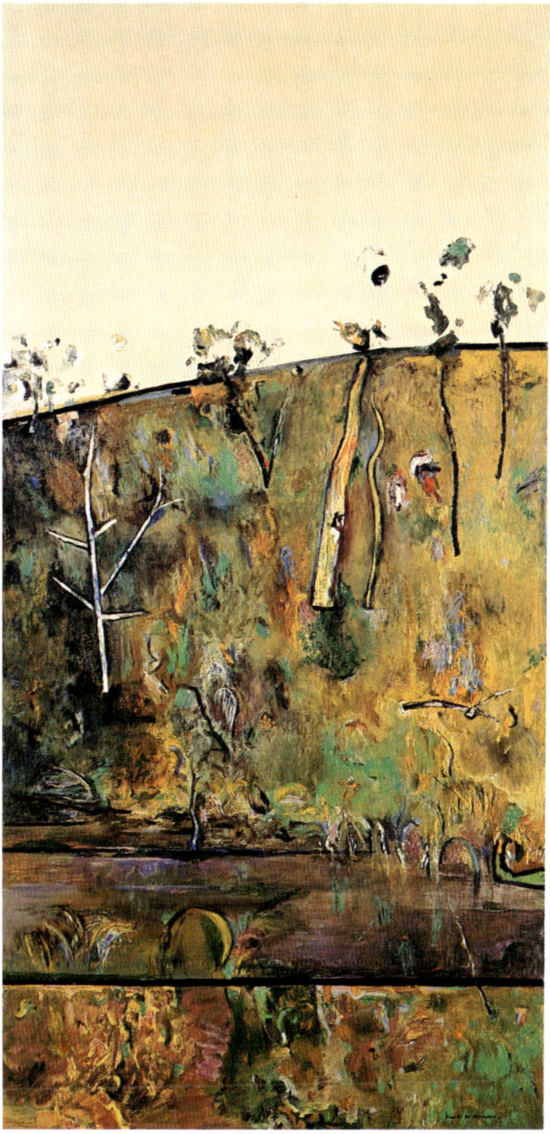

Fred Williams
Australia Vic. 1927–82
Yan Yean 1970
Oil on canvas
207.5 x 104.5cm
Purchased 1986 with the assistance of the Queensland Art Gallery Foundation

Williams's development of a unique and significant vision of landscape in this country has had a profound influence on Australian painting. Yan Yean *is an important 'linking' work, including elements of Williams's minimalist paintings in the Hillside and Hummock series and the Upwey landscapes. It also prefigures the pearly colourations of his last Pilbara works.* Yan Yean *depicts a place in the Dandenong mountains near Melbourne.*

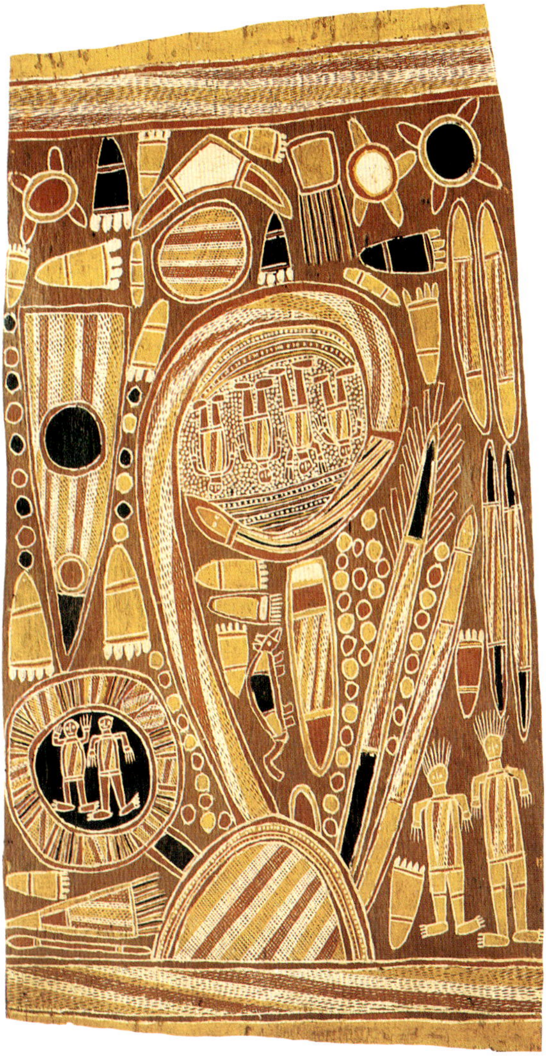

Dawidi Djulwarak
Australia WA 1921–70
Wagilag Sisters c.1970
Natural pigments on bark
114.3 x 63.5cm
Purchased 1971

The story depicted in this painting is the basis of one of the major Aboriginal religious cycles in Arnhem Land. The Wagilag Sisters were ancestral beings who travelled through the region naming hills, springs and other parts of the landscape. This painting traces their travels and actions which culminated in the Sisters angering Wititj the Rainbow Serpent, who swallowed them and their two children. The four bodies, surrounded by Wititj, are at the centre of the painting.

images and signs. In *Triptych: Requiem, Of Grandeur, Empire* 1989 he challenges the patriarchal, Eurocentric interpretation of Australian history and culture. The schematic representation of one-point perspective is incorporated as both a symbol of the European way of seeing things and a painter's technique. A second schema, the dot painting technique used by the traditional central and western desert artists, overlays all three paintings and restates the artist's dual cultural and artistic heritage. Similarly, the photographs of Leah King-Smith explore 'patterns of connection' in her retrieval of Aboriginal history.

Many contemporary artists refer to and incorporate photographic imagery in their work. Photography-based techniques are often employed in screenprinting. The poster *Never was so much owed to so many by so few*, made by James Swan at Brisbane's Griffith University in 1980, is titled by inverting Winston Churchill's statement on the fighter pilots in the Battle of Britain. This work is a witty reminder of the significant role played by posters at this time in Queensland's political history. The vibrantly-coloured, photo-montaged screenprinting technique seen in this work featured strongly in Australian political posters during the 1980s.

Internationally, a number of artists working in photography are extending the parameters of this medium in explorative ways. Australian photographers, including Jacky Redgate, Robyn Stacey, Jay Younger and Anne Zahalka, are reinforcing the prominent position currently occupied by women photographers. Marian Drew's large format, type C colour photographs investigate the possibilities of the manipulation of evocative imagery. In *Late fall* 1989 from her 'New York' series, she incorporates the element of time as she traces with the camera her own physical interaction with the various materials and images assembled in her studio for this photograph.

In contrast, the familiar realities of everyday life fall under the watchful eyes of other artists. The gelatin silver (black and white) photographs of Queenslander Glen O'Malley, such as *Sideburn scramble* 1971, reflect an interest in capturing (almost in a social documentary style) the casual aspects of everyday existence, as these nostalgic visual snippets become understated triggers for wider understandings about our lives.

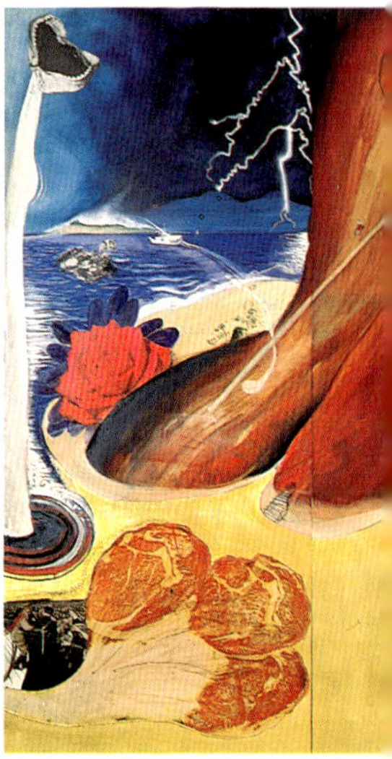

In his installation piece *Day in day out (second version)* 1991, Aleks Danko continues this concern with everyday life. He creates a microcosm of the clockwork regularity of the daily cycles of suburban life, using the ephemeral and temporary quality of moving light projected onto a vast ordered arrangement of miniature cast aluminium 'houses'.

For many contemporary artists, it is the physicality of actual materials that is central to the art-making process. Over the last two decades, studio-glass artists have come to prominence in the Australian art world. The craft-based glass-blowing techniques initiated in the 1970s were joined in the 1980s by techniques which explored the manipulation of glass within a creative context. Artist Judi Elliott played a significant role in this development. Elliott has adapted her experience as a ceramic artist to the newly introduced techniques of fused and slumped glass, as evident in her vibrantly patterned and coloured work *Platter: . . . of how things are* 1988.

Worn, weathered and recycled materials were chosen by Tom Risley to create his *White beech chair* 1988–89. This work prompts the viewer's imagination and evokes memories of surface and experience. Over the past ten years, Risley has extended the concept of 'truth to materials' to its farthest extreme as he reinterprets a wealth of materials including driftwood, rubber thongs, dismembered car bonnets and weatherboards salvaged from demolished Queensland houses.

Like Risley, Rosalie Gascoigne is a *bricoleur*, someone who creates an object, not necessarily functional, by dismantling, arranging and/or reassembling pre-existing objects of entirely different intent and function. Both artists work intimately

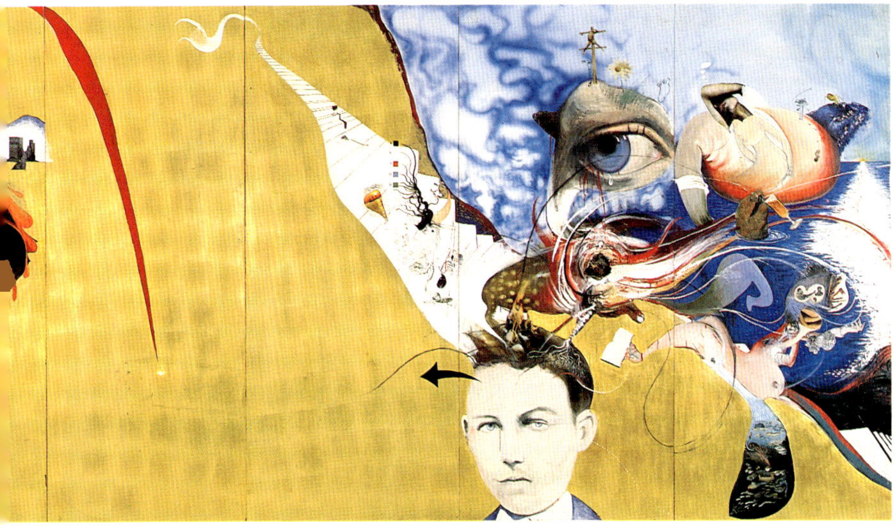

Brett Whiteley
Australia NSW 1939–92
Portrait of Arthur Rimbaud 1970–71
Mixed media with mummified lacquered cat's head on board
203.3 x 518.1 cm
Purchased 1977

Arthur Rimbaud was a rebellious nineteenth-century French poet whose extremely individual approach to life, passion and art offered direct inspiration for Whiteley. Some of the imagery and much of the spirit of Rimbaud's A Season in Hell *has been included in this portrait. The artist himself has been posthumously celebrated as much as the symbolist poet.*

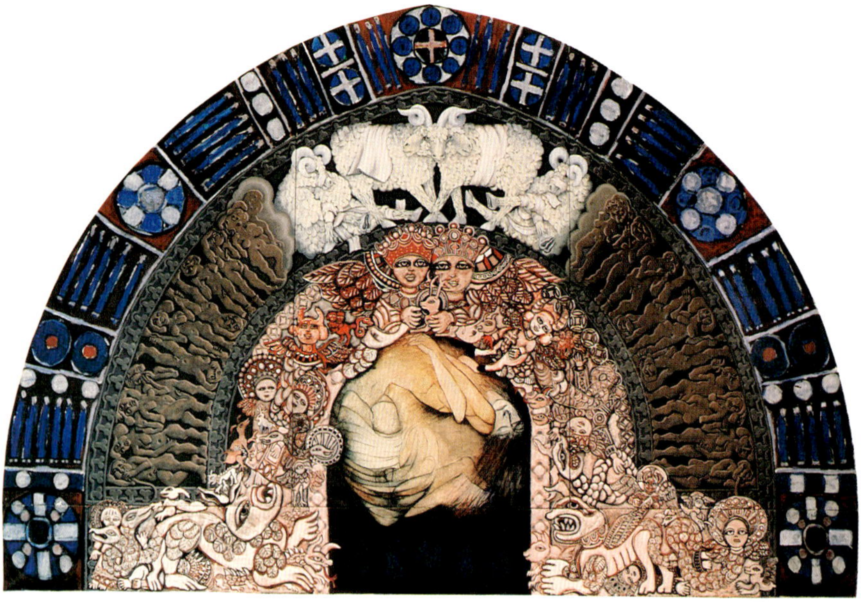

George Baldessin
Australia Vic. 1939–78
Roger Kemp
Australia Vic. 1908–1987
Les Kossatz
Australia Vic. b.1943
Mirka Mora
Australia Vic. b.1928
Andrew Sibley
Australia Vic. b.1933
Tympan 1977
Oil on canvas
Four panels: 424 x 630cm
(overall, irreg.)
Purchased 1991. Queensland
Art Gallery Foundation

The collaborative nature of Gothic architecture and the multicultural character of Australia resonate in this painting: Baldessin was born in Italy, Mora in France and Sibley in England, while Kossatz (of Slavonic descent) and Kemp were both born in Melbourne. Before commencing work, the architectural form of a cathedral tympanum was chosen and the allocation of spaces was decided. The outside 'frame' was painted by Kemp, the next inner space by Sibley, the 'keystone' by Kossatz, the remainder of the arc by Mora, and the central space by Baldessin.

with aged materials which in turn possess and communicate their own untold history. In *Lamp lit* 1989, Gascoigne has collected and collaged yellow light-reflective road signs into a visual poem of lines and dislocated words.

Alison Clouston continues this tradition of breathing new life into discarded materials. *Pterodactyl car* 1985 transforms cast-off scraps from the city and the bush into a threatening mechanical monster. The rough, survival-skills construction of this primitive vehicle makes a deliberate departure from the fine art tradition, in order to create sculpture which bluntly engages with such real-life issues as cars and pollution. Beyond the artist's social comment, however, the creature seems to take on a life of its own.

Bronwyn Oliver explores materials and illusion in another way. In *Curlicue* 1991, the woven strands of patinated copper wire hint at a past history of ancient materials. These pieces assume subtle reductionist forms and invite suggestions of an undetermined world of growth, ancient symbolism and spirituality.

Works of art can speak on many levels. The voice of the artist, the physical presence of the work itself and the eyes of the viewer are all significant contributors to the evolving dialogue that informs and questions contemporary art. The works in this selection are not intended to illustrate the current state of art in this country but, rather, to suggest the breadth and diversity of approach taken by artists as they negotiate their dialogue with the world.

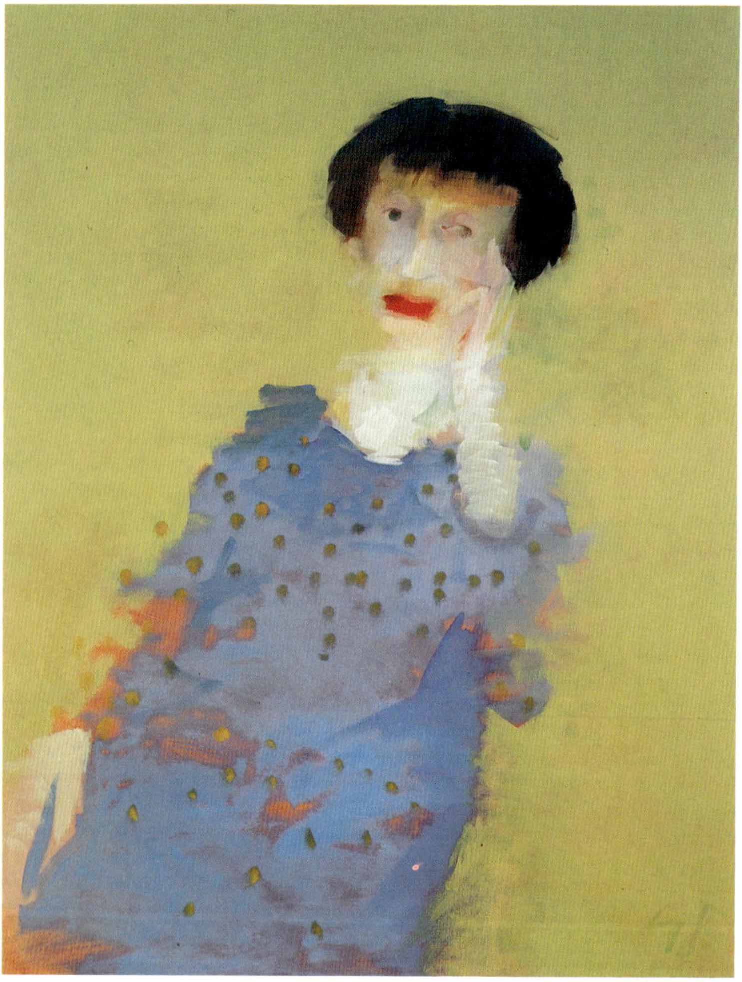

Sam Fullbrook
Australia Qld b.1922
Ernestine Hill 1970
Oil on canvas
96.8 x 76.3 cm
Gift of the artist 1972

Sam Fullbrook and Ernestine Hill shared a similarly independent approach to art and life. During the 1940s and 1950s, Hill was one of Australia's most popular writers, concentrating on journalism, travel writing and historical romance. Her titles include The Great Australian Loneliness *and* My Love Must Wait. *This intimate portrait of Hill reflects Fullbrook's hope of combining tenderness, charm and clarity in his work.*

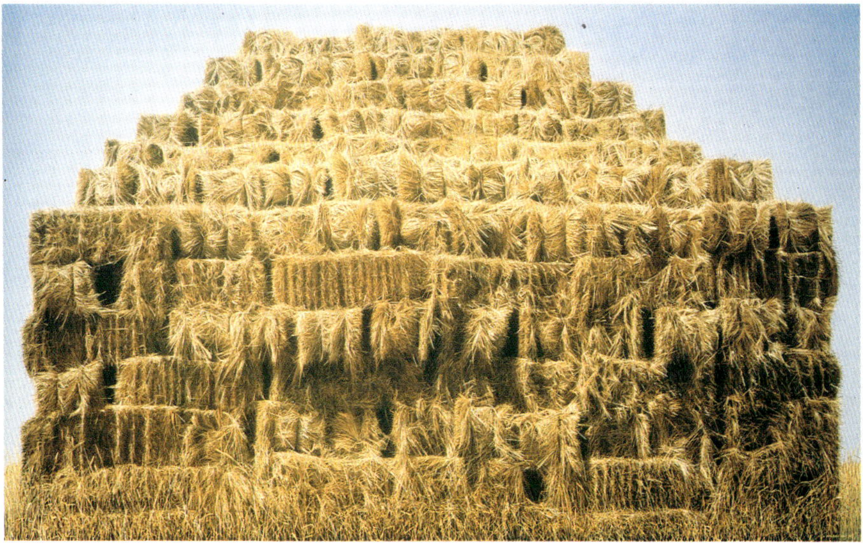

William Delafield Cook
Australia NSW b.1936
A haystack 1982
Synthetic polymer paint on canvas
183 x 305cm
Purchased 1982. Queensland Art Gallery Foundation

Cook's photo-realist paintings first attracted widespread interest in the 1970s. His recent works are a celebration of his subjects, mostly landscapes. A haystack *is the simplest of images, yet densely packed with texture and detail. This large-scale painting is one of the most popular works in the Gallery's Australian collection.*

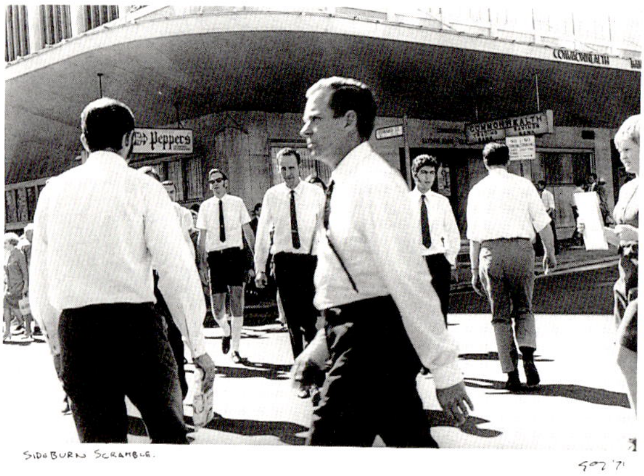

Left
Glen O'Malley
Australia Qld b.1948
Sideburn scramble 1971
Gelatin silver photograph
13.8×20.6cm (comp.)
Purchased 1991. John Darnell Bequest

Since the 1970s, Glen O'Malley has been an important Queensland documentary photographer. His photographs are a record of the passing of time—an unassuming record of the artist's friends, their lifestyles and obsessions. O'Malley's subtle visual observations extend to 'street' photography, and the distinctive and familiar imagery in these black and white works provides an opportunity for memories and nostalgic associations to resurface for both the artist and the viewer.

Right
Bea Maddock
Australia Tas. b.1934
Square 1972
Photo-etching and aquatint
ed. 4/10
76×56cm
Purchased 1990. John Darnell Bequest

Although Maddock has been recognised in recent years as a painter, her printed imagery characterises her sombre, penetrating vision. She began photo-etching in 1971–72, finding that, by using a photographic base, she was quickly able to build complex images directly referring to the world at large. For Square, her source material was a textbook on the study of movement of people in cities. Maddock demonstrates the alienation of the individual in late twentieth-century culture by her use of figures striding in different directions across an urban space.

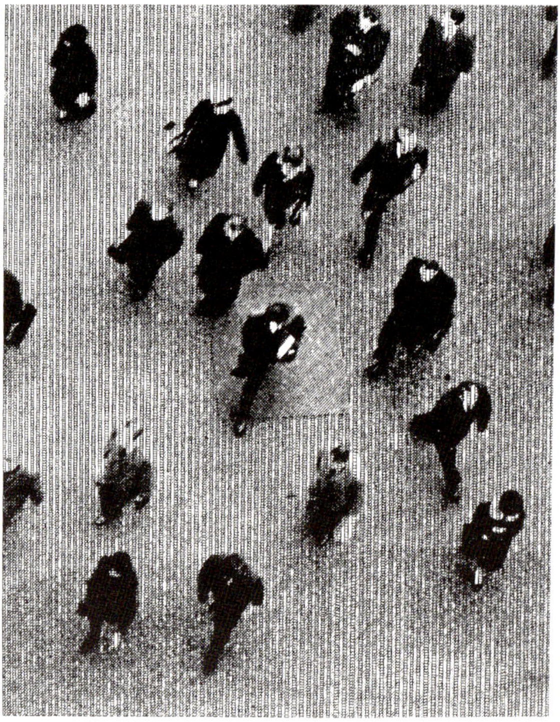

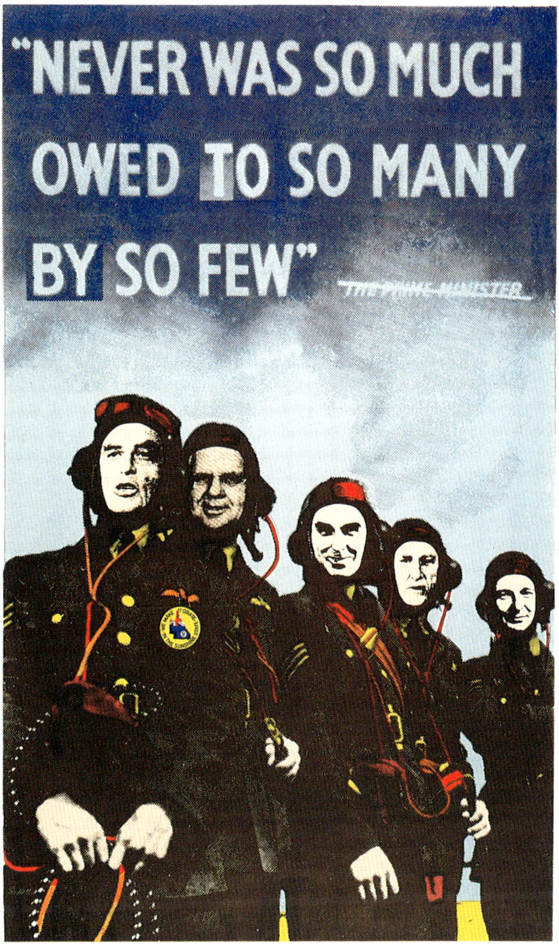

James Swan
Australia Qld b.1959
Never was so much owed to so many by so few 1980
Photo-screenprint
91 x 58cm (comp.)
Purchased 1990. John Darnell Bequest

Former prominent Australian political figures—Sir Joh Bjelke-Petersen, Russell Hinze, Sir Llew Edwards, Malcolm Fraser and Doug Anthony—are caricatured in this work. Like many works created at Griffith University's screenprinting studio (established by Michael Callaghan in 1979), this work incorporates photographic images and cut stencils—techniques used extensively to produce posters of immediate visual power and political influence.

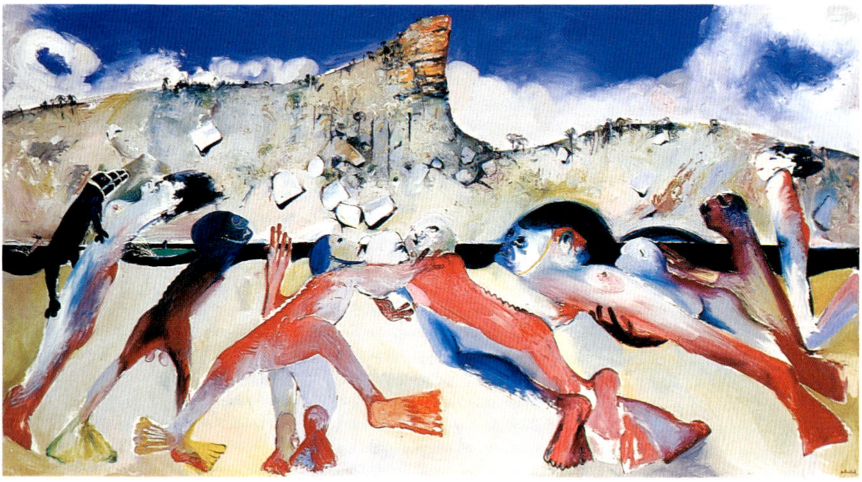

Above
Arthur Boyd
Australia Vic. b.1920
Bathers and Pulpit Rock
1984–85
Oil on canvas
242.3 × 456.2cm
Purchased 1987 with the assistance of Arthur Boyd and Stuart Purves, Australian Galleries

This work compares the classical concept of sport as fitness for war with the Australian pursuit of pleasure through sport and its intrusion into the natural environment. Throughout his career, Boyd has revealed disturbing aspects of humanity often disguised within civilisation. In this painting, the flipper-wearing bathers resemble amphibian monsters invading the landscape.

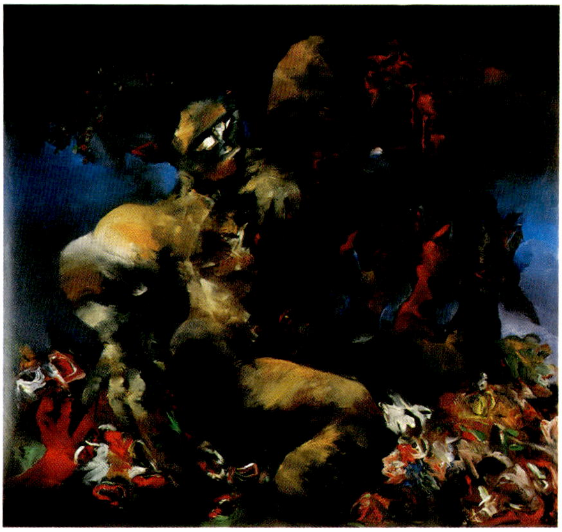

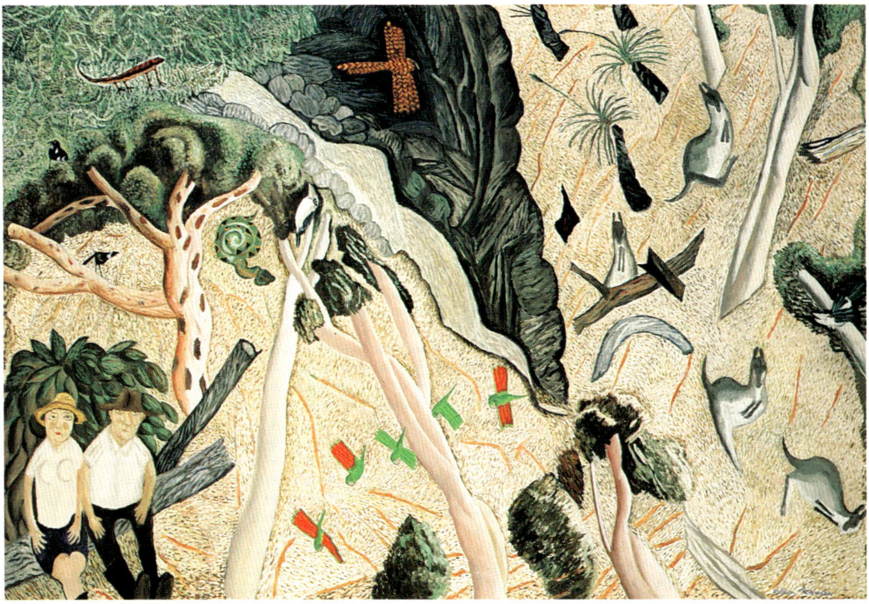

Opposite
Gordon Shepherdson
Australia Qld b.1934
Man climbing over images
1988
Oil and enamel on paper
136.5 x 150cm
Purchased 1990

Shepherdson's expressionist style establishes him as the most significant follower of the expressionist painter Jon Molvig. He has remained consistently true to his initial, albeit sombre, vision: his first exhibition in 1964 was based on images of the slaughterhouse. His palette has also remained extraordinarily consistent. Shepherdson works passionately and intuitively, moving the paint directly with his hands. This work and its companion piece Man with 54 years of masks *are, as their titles suggest, largely autobiographical.*

Above
William Robinson
Australia Qld b.1936
William and Shirley, flora and fauna 1985
Oil on canvas
126 x 187cm
Purchased 1985

This work is a portrait of the artist and his wife surrounded by the landscape of the Gold Coast hinterland where they were living at the time. Robinson's paintings invite the viewer to take a joyous journey of discovery through his delicate brushwork, complex colour and touches of humour. The illusion of the revolving vista created by simultaneous multiple viewpoints is a device which suggests the universal and fragile beauty of nature.

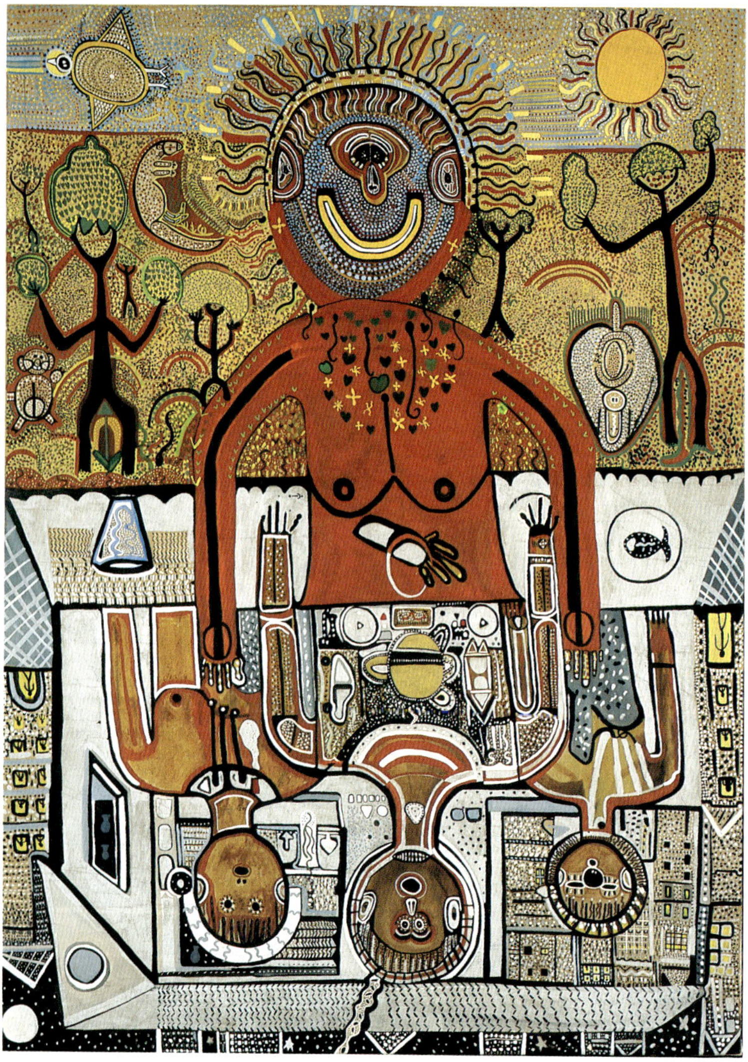

Trevor Nickolls
Australia SA b.1949
From Dreamtime 2 Machinetime 1979
Oil on canvas
161.3 x 117.6cm
Purchased 1989 under the Contemporary Art Acquisition Program with funds from Brian and Rosemary White through the Queensland Art Gallery Foundation

Trevor Nickolls is an Aboriginal artist from Adelaide whose work explores the complex issue of dual heritage. He does not claim an extensive knowledge of traditions, way of life or meaning behind the art of his ancestors, apart from what he knows by intuition. He was the first widely recognised, urban Aboriginal artist, and his work on the theme Dreamtime/Machinetime is a balancing act—a tightrope walked between his dreams and his life in urban society.

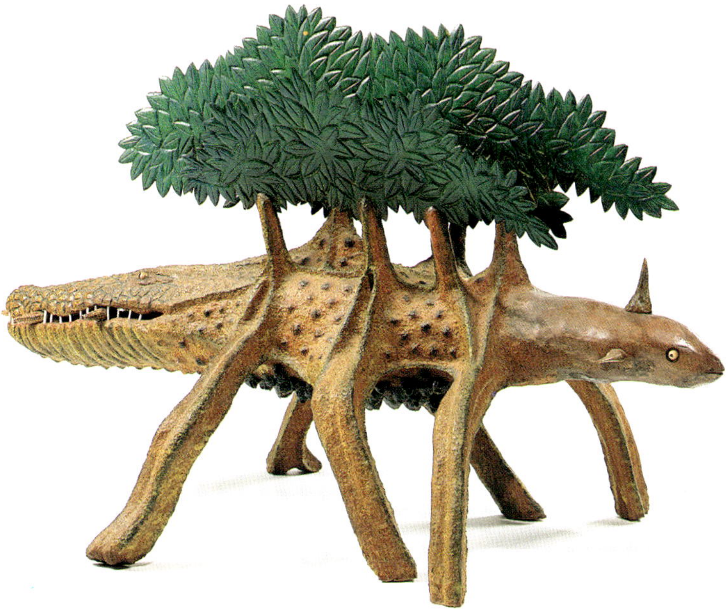

William Yaxley
Australia Qld b.1943
The mangrove monster no. 2 1986
Mixed media
90 x 87 x 146cm
Purchased 1987

Yaxley's exuberant creations reflect his highly imaginative vision. In this sculpture, Yaxley has combined timber, shells, paint, resin and treated mandarin skins, gathered on his farm on the central Queensland coast. The densely textured 'monster' suggests a sinister salamander, a maternal alligator or a fantastic spirit, emerging semi-evolved from an imagined primordial landscape.

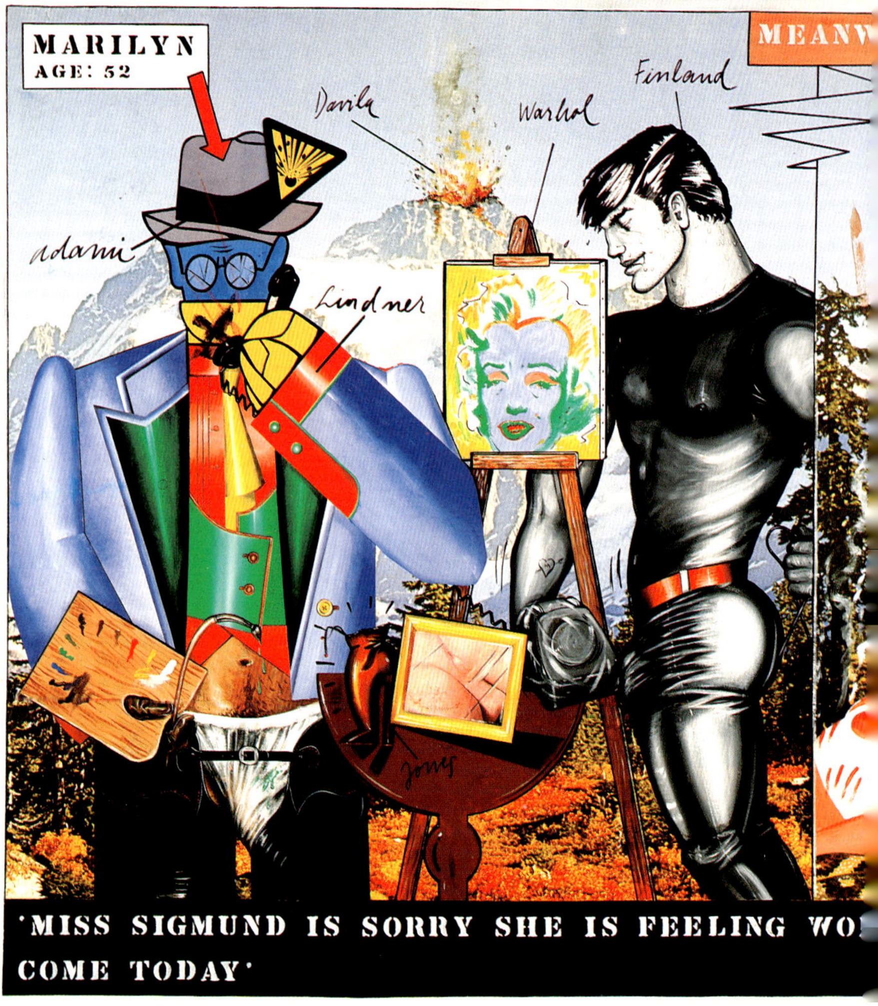
MARILYN
AGE: 52
MEANW
Davila
Warhol
Finland
adami
Lindner
Jones
'MISS SIGMUND IS SORRY SHE IS FEELING WO
COME TODAY'

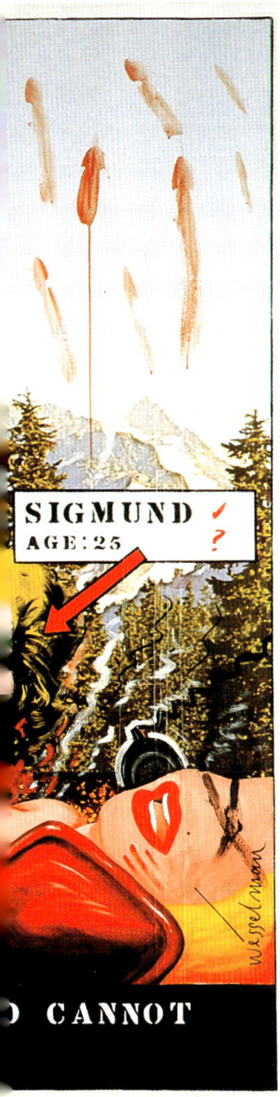

Juan Davila
Australia Vic. b.1946
Miss Sigmund 1981
Synthetic polymer paint
on photographic mural
200 × 260.5cm
Purchased 1991 with funds
from the 1990 International
Exhibitions Program

The art of Chilean-born Davila embraces cultural politics, sexuality, social identity and the simulated reality of the mass media. In Miss Sigmund, *a 'tasteless' photographic mural forms the backdrop for a myriad of painted quotations from the works of other artists, including Adami's portrait of Sigmund Freud, a Wesselman nude, a Warhol* Marilyn, *a fetishistic stiletto and images from homo-erotic cartoons.*

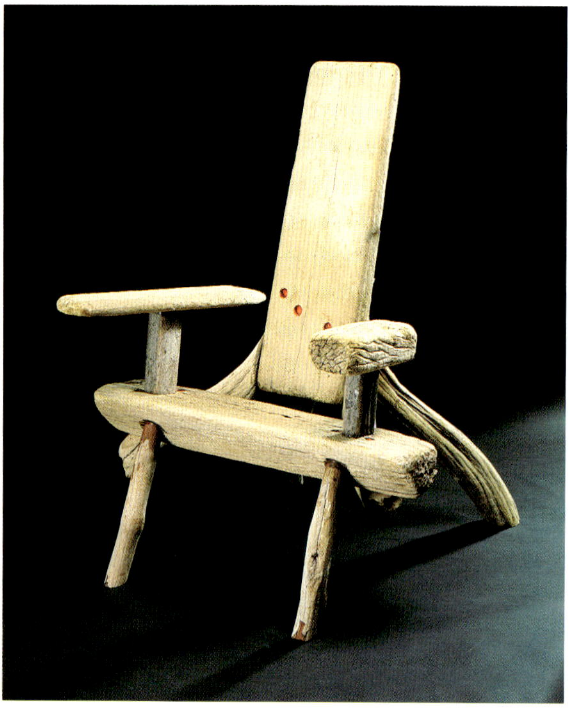

Left
Tom Risley
Australia Qld b.1947
White beech chair 1988–89
White beech driftwood
assembled and bolted
129 x 98 x 130cm
Purchased 1989

Risley uses his trade skills, imaginative eye and whimsical humour to create work from unexpected combinations of found objects. Driftwood that is worn and weathered by the natural elements, part of the flotsam and jetsam found on Queensland beaches, has been transformed by Risley into an inventive series of furniture works including White beech chair.

Right
Alison Clouston
Australia NSW b.1957
Pterodactyl car 1985
Galvanised iron, timber and
found objects
183 x 366 x 549cm
Purchased 1991. Queensland
Art Gallery Functions Fund

This witty and bizarre construction has a very specific socio-ecological meaning. As well as being a fantasy creature for flights of the imagination, the Pterodactyl car *is a comment on the mindless consumption of natural resources and human lives by our automobile culture. This imaginary survivor of some post petrol-engine apocalypse is quite literally a vehicle for the viewer's thoughts.*

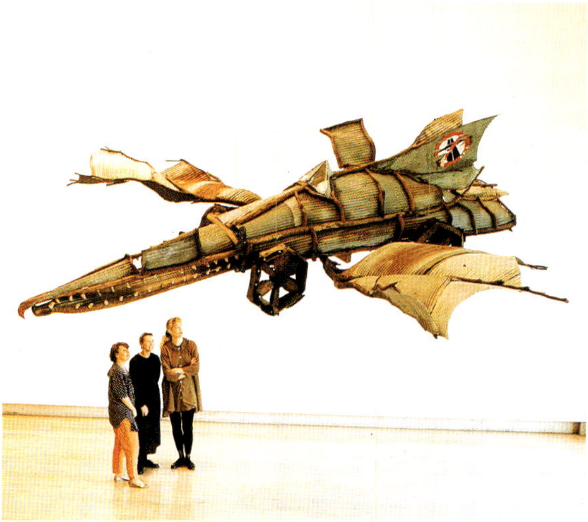

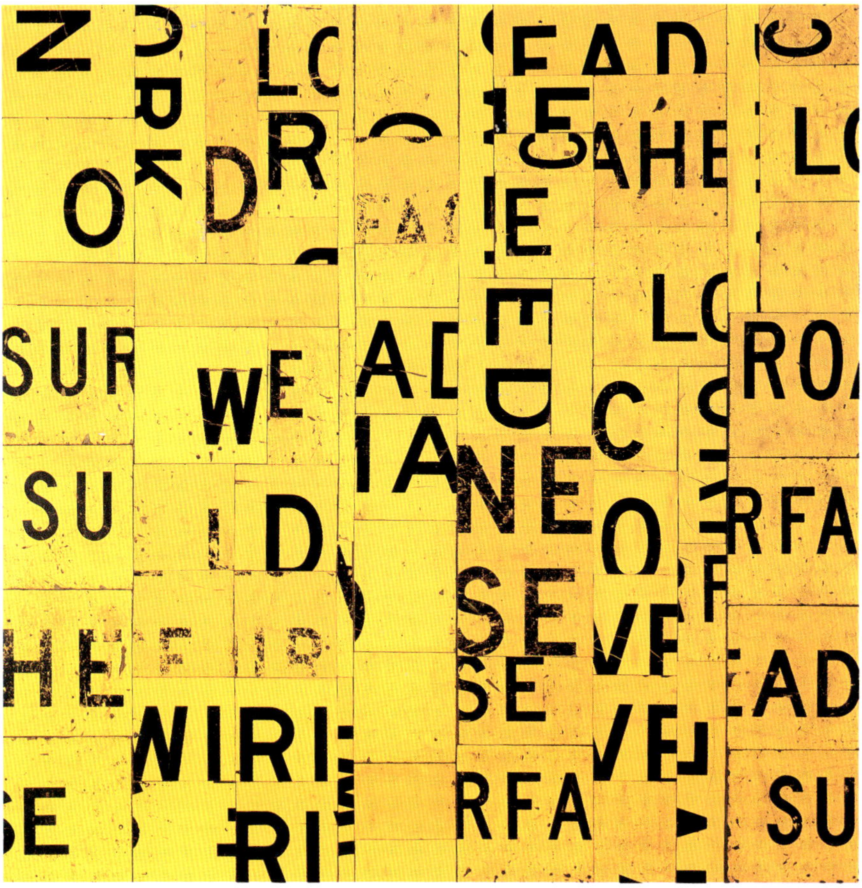

Rosalie Gascoigne
Australia ACT b.1917
Lamp lit 1989
Retro-reflective road signs on board
183 x 183cm
Purchased 1990. Mrs J.R. Lucas Estate in memory of her father, John Robertson Blane

Gascoigne's art is assemblage —she brings the detritus of everyday life into new aesthetic and poetic contexts. Lamp lit *is constructed from cut and carefully recomposed reflective road signs. This material may trigger memories of long-distance road travel; but for the artist, the yellow reminded her of a profusion of roadside flowers seen outside her hometown of Canberra.*

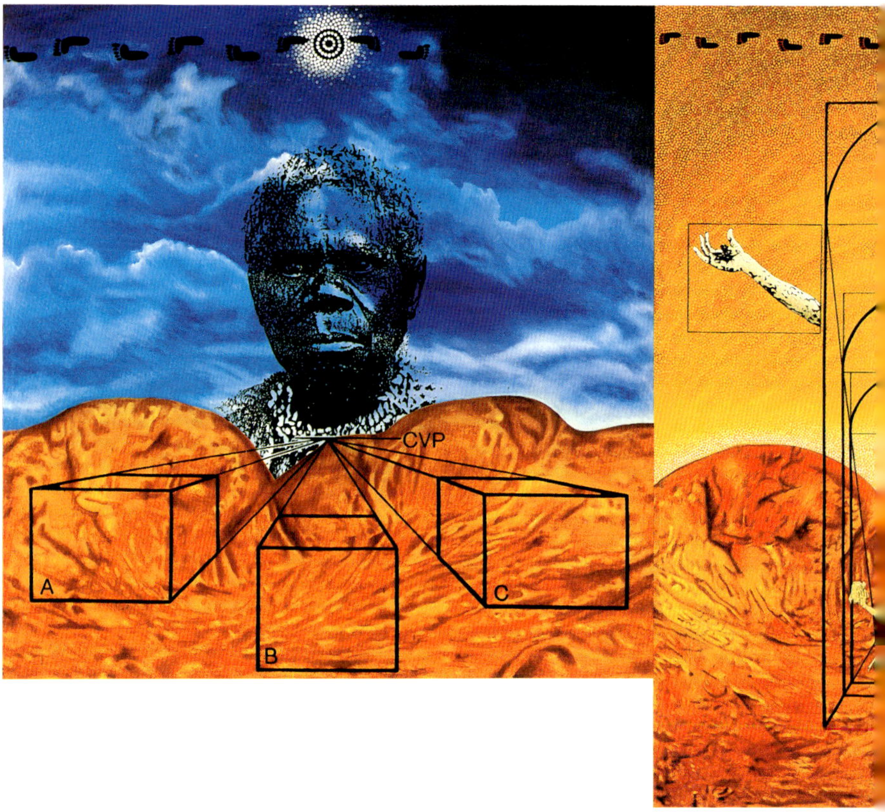
CVP
A
B
C

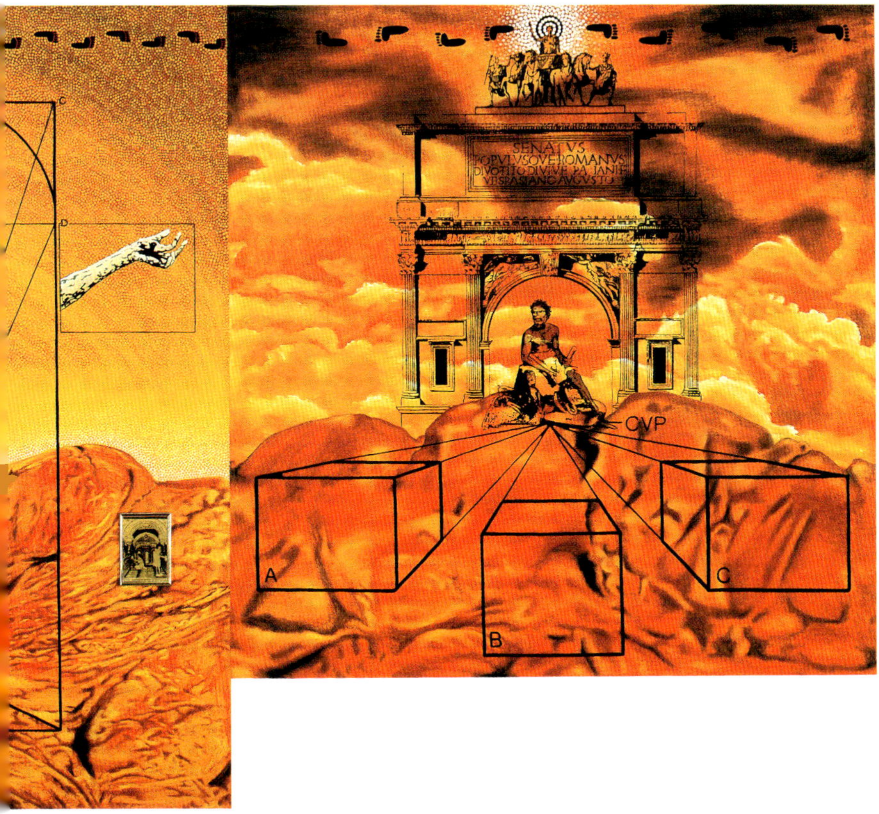

Gordon Bennett
Australia Qld b.1955
Triptych: Requiem, Of Grandeur, Empire 1989
Oil and photograph on canvas
a: 120 × 120cm; b: 200 × 150cm; c: 120 × 120cm
Purchased 1989 under the Contemporary Art Acquisition Program with funds from Hill & Taylor, Solicitors, through the Queensland Art Gallery Foundation

Bennett addresses critical issues of Aboriginality in Australia through a post-modern visual language of appropriation and cultural references. In Requiem, *Truganini's face gazes at the viewer, a haunting reminder of the massacre and exile of Tasmanian Aborigines.* Of Grandeur *links the Christian symbol of martyrdom with an early magazine photograph of the artist's mother. In* Empire, *an image of Rome's Arch of Titus looms over a landscape of death.*

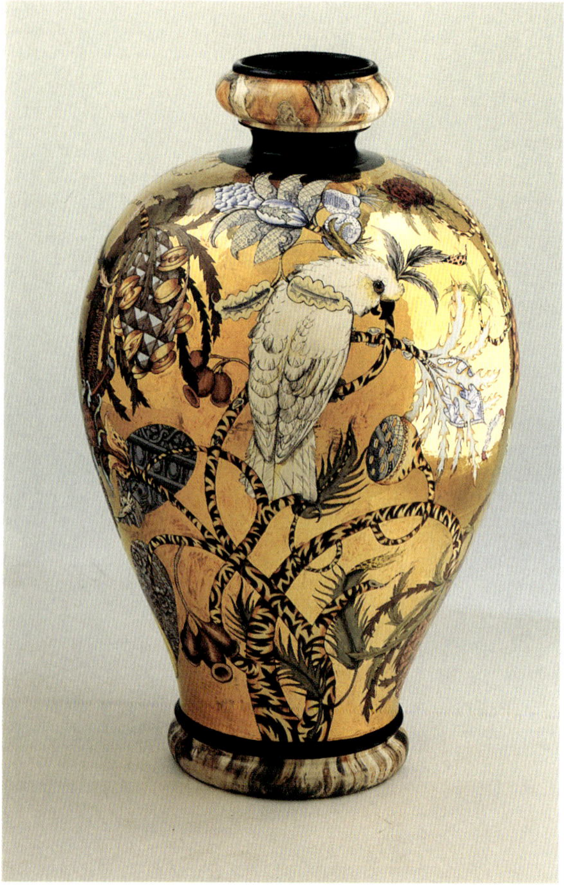

Left
Stephen Bowers
Australia SA b.1953
Mark Heidenreich
Australia NSW b.1958
Vase: Chintz 1990
Stoneware and gold lustre
85 x 56cm (diam.)
Purchased 1991. Queensland Art Gallery Foundation

This thrown baluster vase was formed by Heidenreich, while the complex painted decoration was applied by Bowers. Decorative arts history is quoted in Bowers's version of the 'willow pattern', which features Sydney's Harbour Bridge and Opera House. Architectural fragments, a cockatoo, foliate sprays, and gum leaves and gumnuts direct from the illustrations of May Gibbs's Australian children's classic Snugglepot and Cuddlepie complete the highly ornate decoration.

Right
Judi Elliott
Australia NSW b.1934
Platter: . . . of how things are 1988
Slumped glass mosaic
10 x 53 x 53cm
Gift of the Queensland Art Gallery Society 1989

Elliott was a prominent ceramist before she enrolled in the glass design course at the Canberra School of Art under the German glass-worker Klaus Moje. The techniques of kiln forming and slumping used in this platter are typical of the work produced at the school. However, Elliott's facility with brilliant colour and geometric structures create a distinctive character in her work.

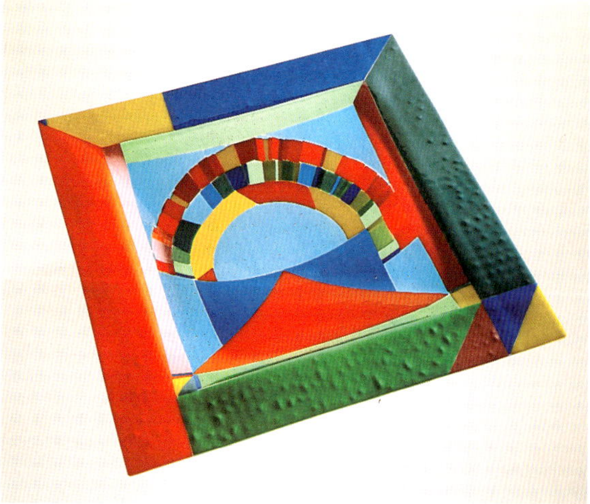

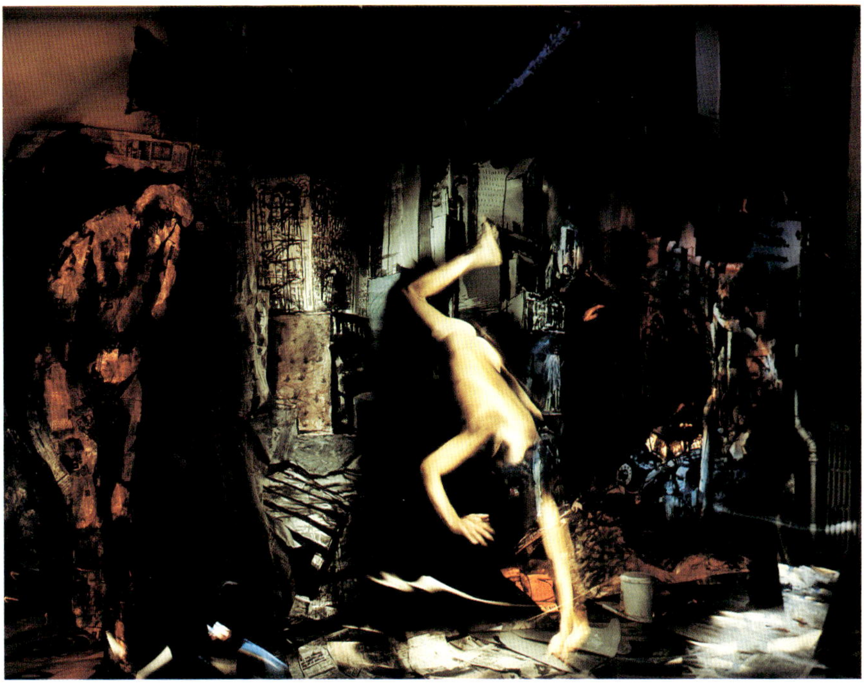

Marian Drew
Australia Qld b.1960
Late fall 1989
Type C photograph
97.3 x 128.5cm (comp.)
Purchased 1990. Queensland Art Gallery Society

An accomplished exponent of experimental photography, Queenslander Marian Drew builds environments of objects, collage and drawing, before documenting them on film. Ephemeral installations and fleeting gestures characterise the end results. The painted figure at the left of Late fall *is strongly reminiscent of Masaccio's* Adam and Eve *and brings with it a sense of shame, fear and loss. It is combined with the falling naked figure to reflect the atmosphere of desperation, tension and vulnerability of our urban environment.*

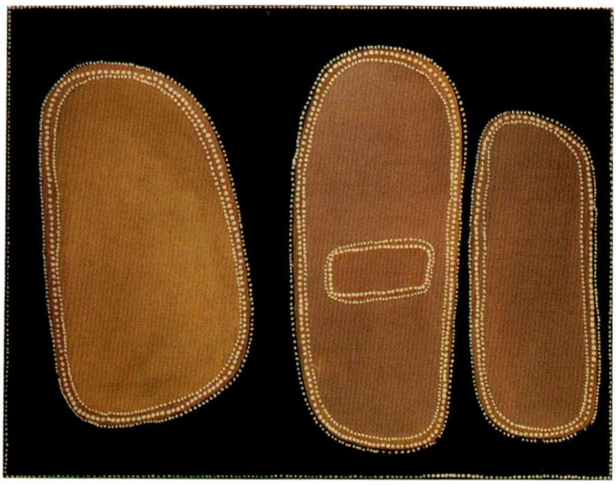

Left
Rover Thomas
Australia WA b.1926
Barramundi Dreaming
1989
Natural pigments on canvas
120 x 160cm
Purchased 1994

Like much Aboriginal art from the desert, Barramundi Dreaming *is simultaneously a map, a narrative and a mythological emblem. Essentially a personal form of landscape painting, Thomas's work evokes the stark and rocky topography of the Kimberley district of Western Australia. Rover Thomas's paintings are a new form of cultural expression which began in the 1980s, an extension of an existing tradition of ceremonial body painting in the Kimberley.*

Right
Dolly Nampijinpa Daniels
Australia NT b.1931
Bush Grain Dreaming (Watiyawarnu Jukurrpa)
1990
Synthetic polymer paint on canvas
121.5 x 121.5cm
Purchased 1993. Queensland Art Gallery Foundation

The Aboriginal people of Yuendumu, north-west of Alice Springs in central Australia, continue the tradition of representing their Dreamings through art. These images are adapted from ceremonial ground paintings and body designs. The story represented by this painting involves the travelling associated with seed gathering (bush grain is the seed of an acacia plant, collected and crushed to make flour). On one level, the painting deals with food and the management of resources, but there is also a religious significance in the relationship between people and land in Aboriginal life.

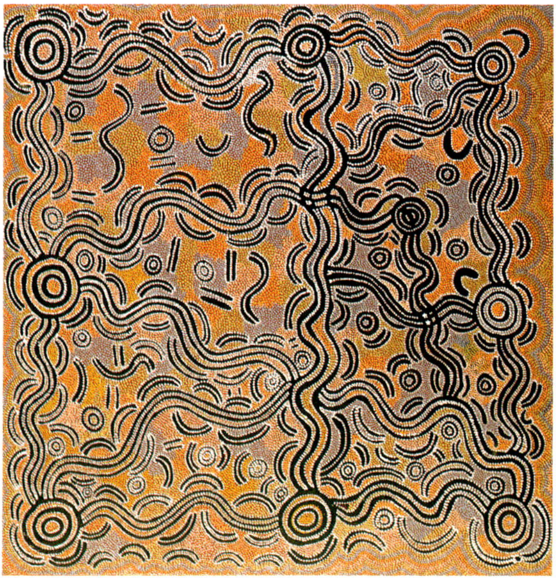

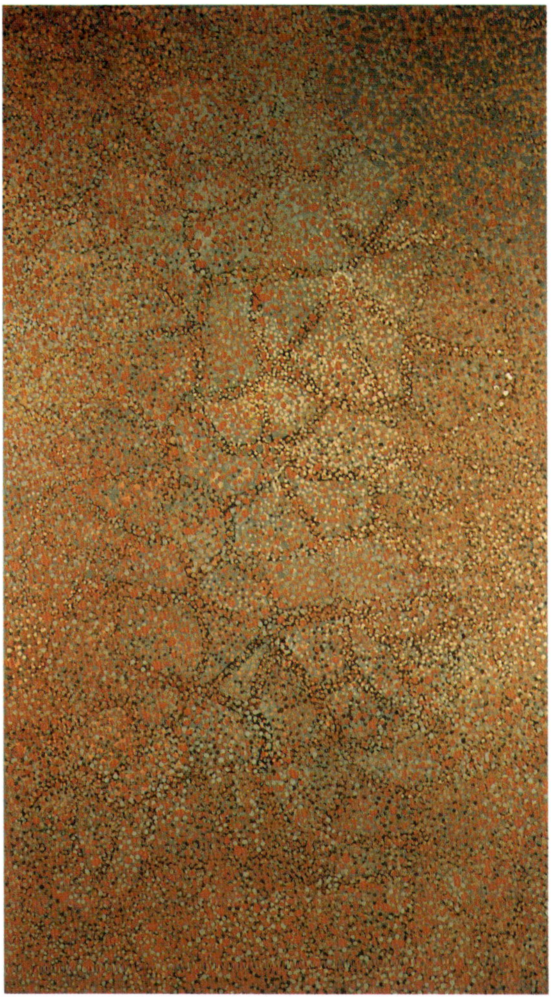

Emily Kame Kngwarreye
Australia NT c.1908
Wild Potato Dreaming
1990
Synthetic polymer paint on canvas
185 x 150cm
Purchased 1990 through the Queensland Art Gallery Foundation

The muted earth colours, limited tonal range and broken surface of Wild Potato Dreaming *evoke a dusty, hazy landscape. It appears as though some elusive subject is veiled by an intermediate surface. Emily Kngwarreye's middle name, Kame, means seed of the* atnulare *(yam or wild potato).* Wild Potato Dreaming *contains references to places in the artist's clan territory where the wild potatoes grow.*

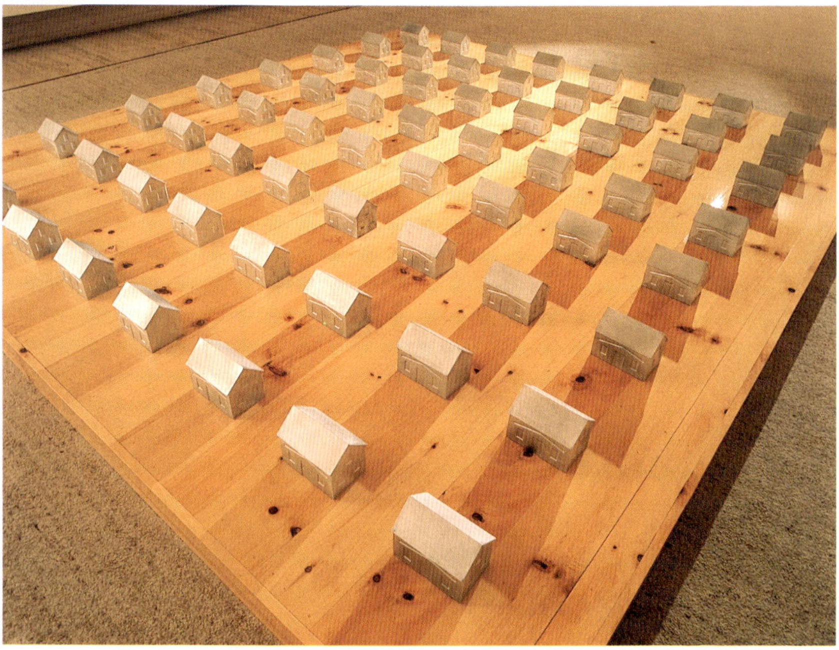

Aleks Danko
Australia NSW b.1950
Day in day out (second version) 1991
Cast aluminium and theatre light on metal support
11 × 260 × 229cm
Purchased 1992

During the 1960s and 1970s, Danko was one of a group of Australian artists who explored the dynamic possibilities of happenings and performance art. Much of his floor-based work explores the alienation the individual experiences in suburban life. Installations such as Day in day out (second version) *suggest the regimentation and sameness of the lives of people working in an industrial society.*

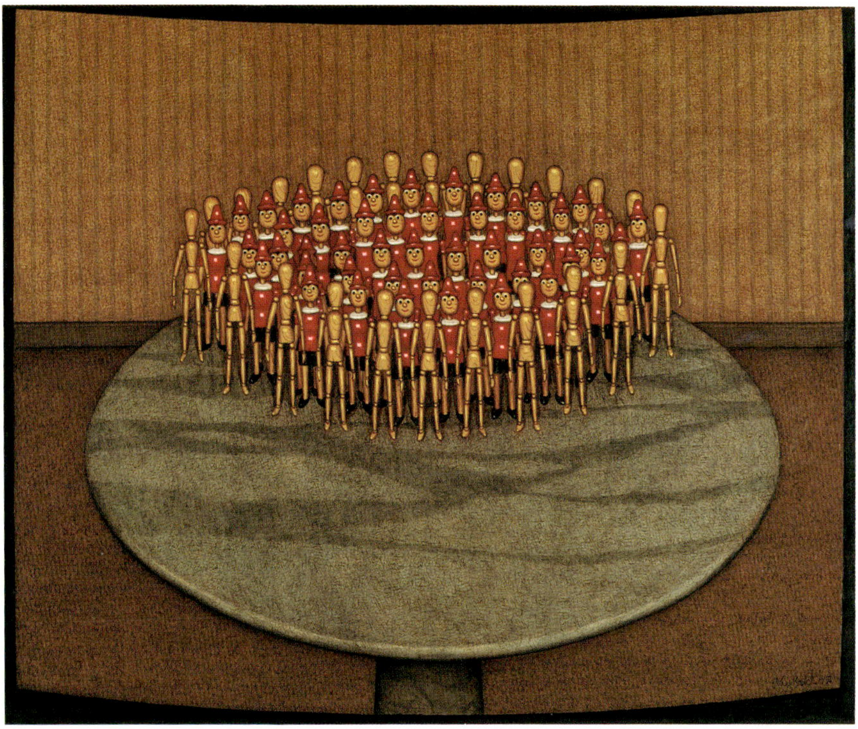

John Brack
Australia Vic. b.1920
Finale 1992
Oil on canvas
109.3 x 136cm
Purchased 1993. Queensland Art Gallery Foundation

In Finale, humanity is represented by a densely packed still life of anonymous, inanimate figures which perform an eerie mechanical ballet. The precise rendering of this crowded scene combines two of the major themes of Brack's oeuvre: the intense study of implements or objects and his fascination with, yet distaste for, crowds. Brack finds a sinister dimension in the prospect of individuality being lost when people think and act with absolute conformity.

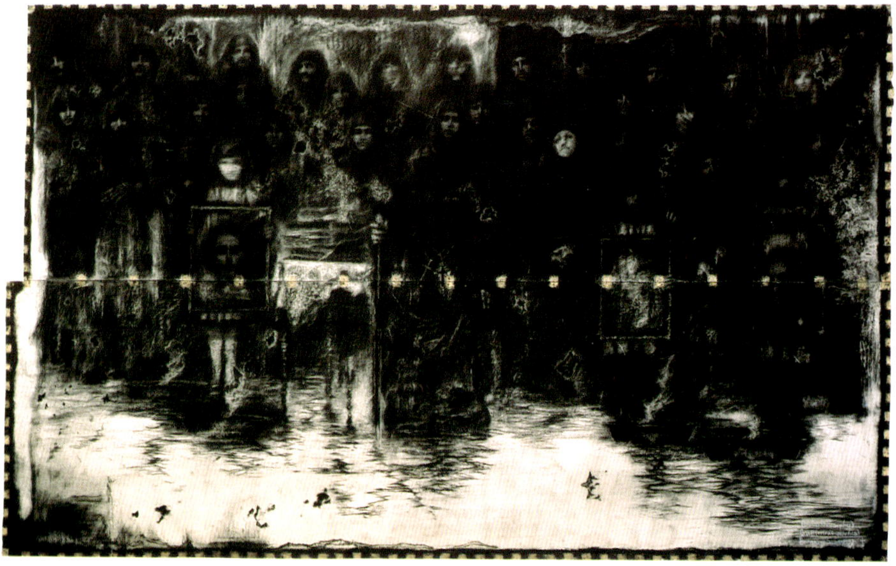

Above
Bernhard Sachs
Australia SA b.1954
During philosophy—group portrait with head 1990
Charcoal
Two sheets: 300 x 500cm (comp.)
Purchased 1990. Queensland Art Gallery Functions Fund

Sachs's huge charcoal drawing parallels the psychoanalytical concerns of a number of Australian artists, including Mike Parr. It combines a procession-like group of figures with the image of St Veronica's veil, said to have been imprinted with the likeness of Christ when she dried his face with it. This work could be described as an extended meditation on transience and mortality.

Opposite
Leah King-Smith
Australia Vic. b.1957
***Untitled I* (from 'Patterns of connection' series)** 1991
Direct positive colour photograph
105 x 116.5cm (comp.)
Purchased 1993. John Darnell Bequest

Leah King-Smith, an artist of Aboriginal descent, retrieves aspects of Aboriginal history by using nineteenth-century photographs. In Untitled I *the enlarged portrait of an Aboriginal girl, Christina Pepper, is superimposed on a landscape, rescuing her image from an archival and ethnographic context. This commanding yet elusive soft-toned photograph conveys a sense not only of the subjection of Australia's indigenous people to colonial forces (indicated by the Victorian dress), but also of their intricate relationship with the land.*

Right
Mike Parr
Australia NSW b.1945
Wax wedge (the trinity of bones) 1991
Synthetic polymer paint, bees wax, margarine on plywood
240 x 360 x 27 cm
Purchased 1994

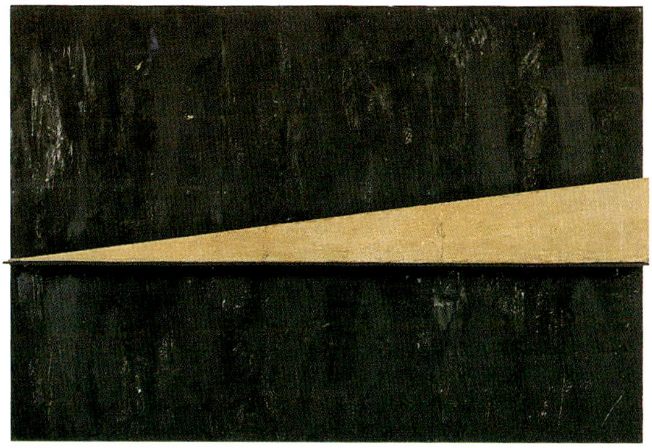

Mike Parr became known as a performance and video artist in the 1970s, using systematic self-mutilation as a metaphor to suggest self-exploration and expression. His Wax wedge (the trinity of bones) *is harshly gouged and burned, carrying the scars from its production. The wedge is a simple form but, as a symbol, it can be read in many ways. It is an implement of penetration and destruction which diminishes to the point of non-existence. Parr makes the wedge a powerful emblem of ambiguity and unease.*

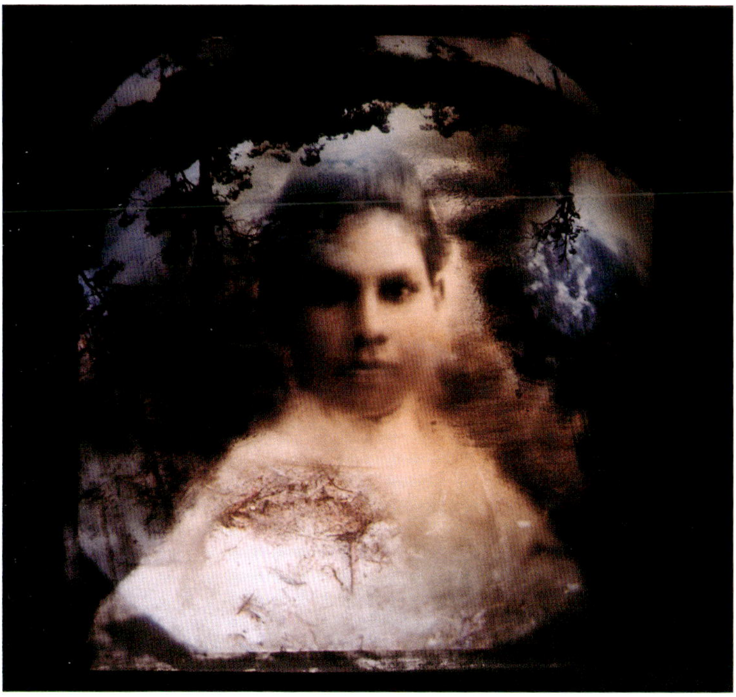

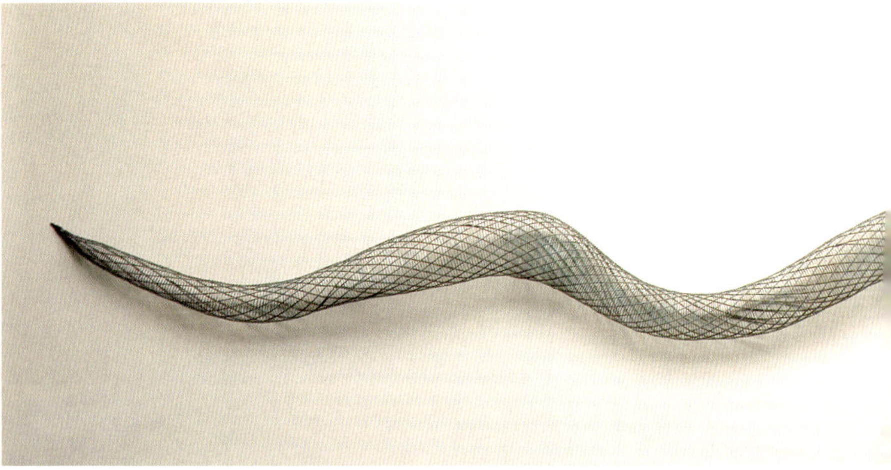

Above
Bronwyn Oliver
Australia NSW b.1959
Curlicue 1991
Copper wire
45 x 250 x 15cm
Purchased 1992. Andrew and Lilian Pedersen Memorial Prize for Small Sculpture 1991 (winning entry)

Bronwyn Oliver's sculptures resemble abstract patterns of growth in their spiralling, swelling and suspension. Curlicue *appears delicate, yet is structurally strong. The patination of the copper obscures the newness of the material and suggests the illusion of being an archaeological discovery. Oliver's sculpture is an attempt to create life, not in the sense of corporeal beings but in the sense of a kind of force or an energy. It is her intention that viewers respond to her works intuitively.*

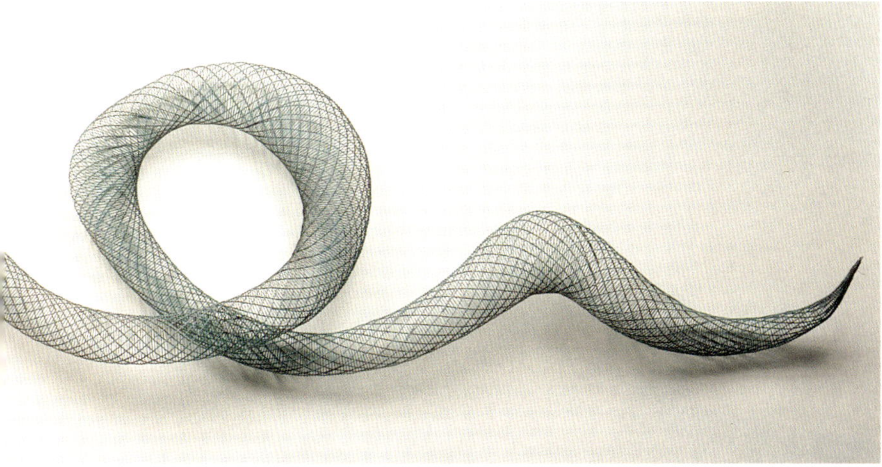

Below
Kathy Temin
Australia Vic. b.1968
White problem #2 1992
Synthetic fur, canvas and stuffing on composition board
Nine parts: 150×63×40cm (each, approx.)
Purchased 1995. Queensland Art Gallery Foundation

This is a bizarre mutation of the pure white, geometric abstract sculptures of minimalist art. Funny and sinister, grubby and vaguely obscene, the sequence of shapes proposes that there cannot be such thing as 'pure form'. Kathy Temin's work implies that, despite the strivings of the most rigorous abstract art, no action or object can be free from hidden meaning.

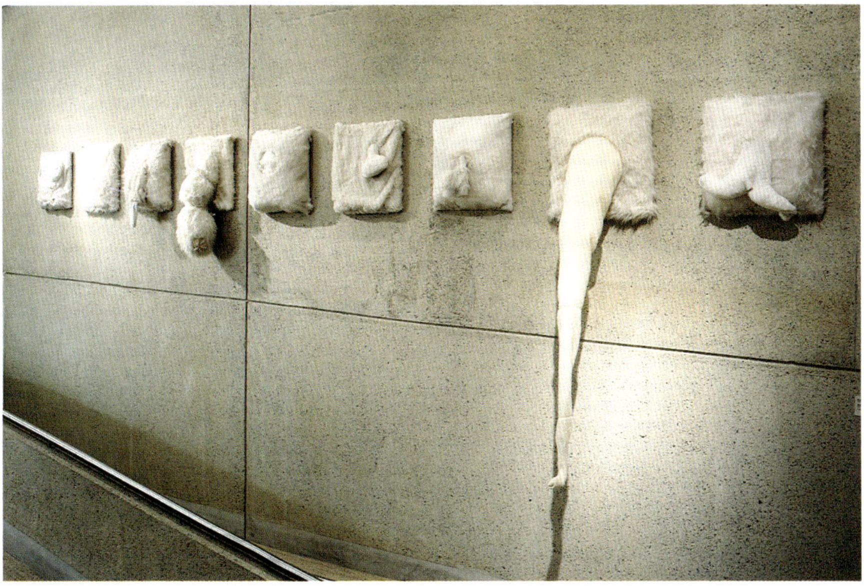

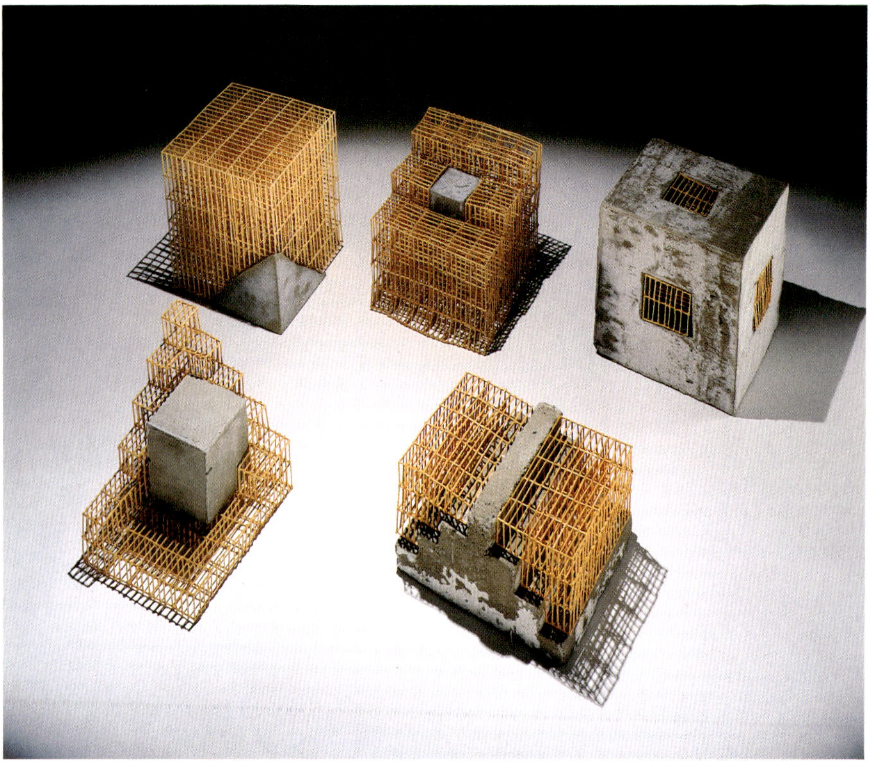

Rodney Spooner
Australia Qld b.1962
Civilised obsession
1992–93
Wood and cement
Five parts: 28 × 28 × 28cm
(each, approx.)
Purchased 1994. Queensland Art Gallery Foundation

These small sculptures of matchsticks and cement refer ironically to the idealistic philosophy of modernism. Spooner's combination of irregular form with a grid structure parodies the rigid geometry of twentieth-century architecture and the notion of building a better world through logic.

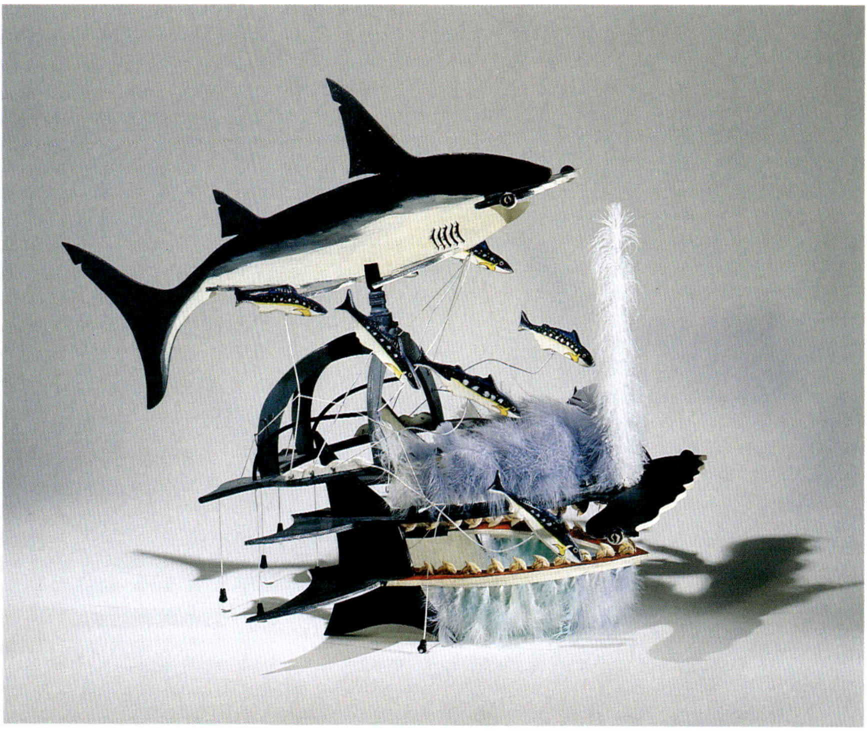

Ken Thaiday
Australia Qld b.1950
Shark mask (with bait fish) 1995
Mixed media
72 x 74 x 67.8cm (approx.)
Purchased 1995. Queensland Art Gallery Foundation

Ken Thaiday was born on Erub Island in Torres Strait. Although he now lives and works on mainland Australia, the celebration of his culture has remained an important aspect of Thaiday's life. The construction of mask-like head-dresses is a traditional art form of the Torres Strait Islands. Thaiday, however, incorporates found materials and creates his own designs rather than adhering to family or clan tradition. This work comprises plywood, wire, feathers, shark teeth and string.

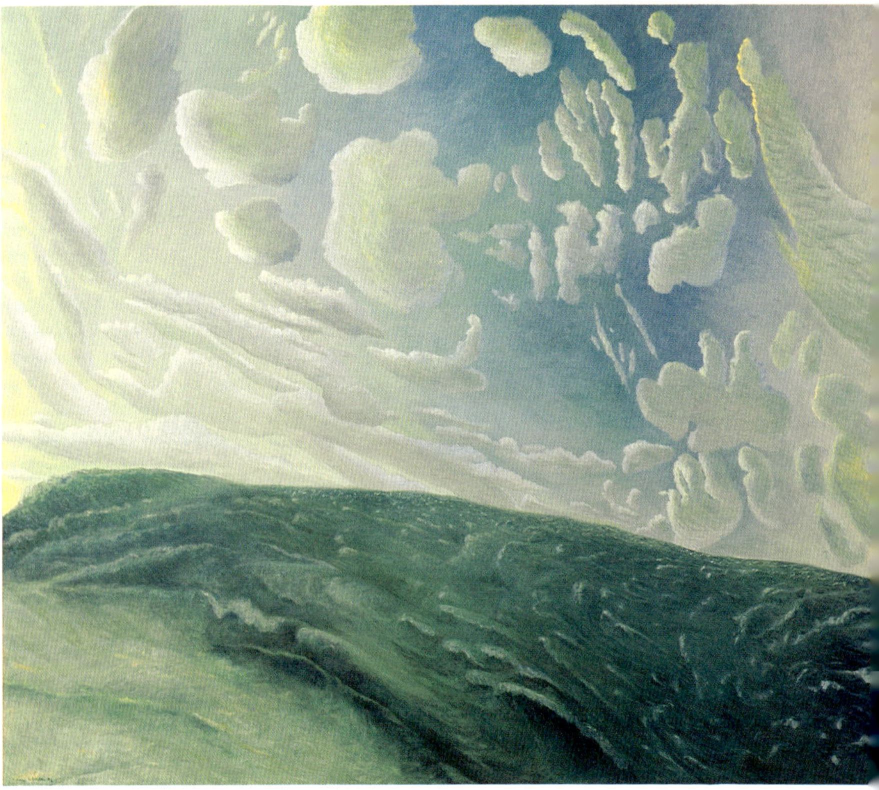

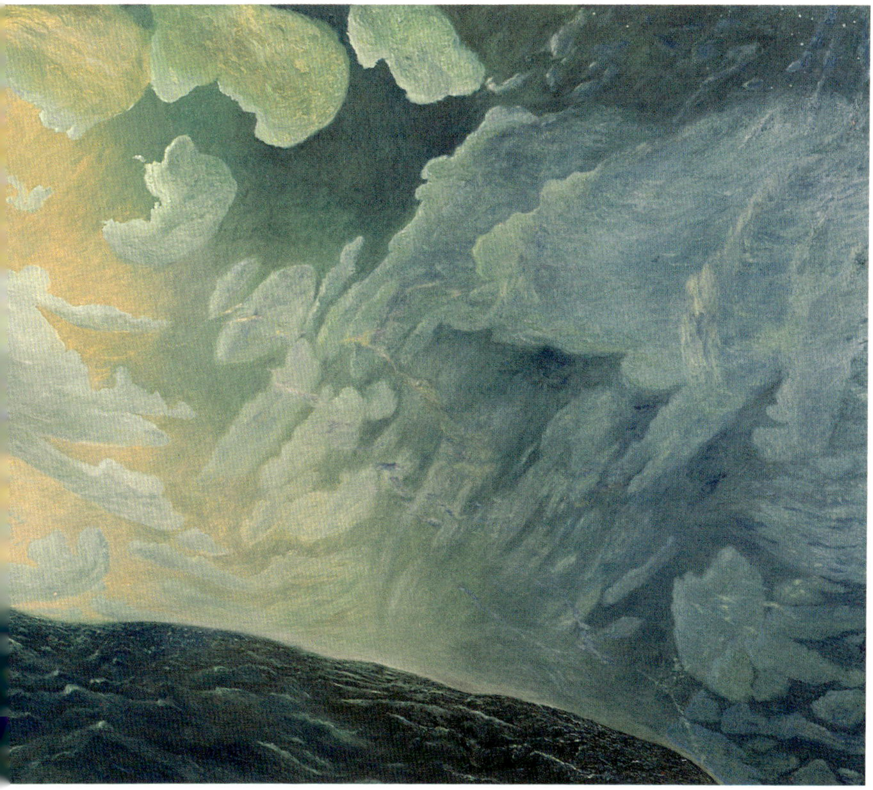

William Robinson
Australia Qld b.1936
Dark tide, Bogangar 1994
Oil on canvas
Diptych: 185 x 446cm (overall)
Purchased 1995 with a special allocation from the Queensland Government. Celebrating the Queensland Art Gallery Centenary 1895–1995

This work represents the artist's first major departure from the subject which was central to his work for a decade, the rainforest 'biospheres' of south-east Queensland. This shift in focus was motivated by Robinson's move from the Gold Coast hinterland to the New South Wales coast. In this painting, the artist eliminates all traces of whimsical detail to depict the dark power of an ocean surge. The shifting perspective, created by planes which recede, tilt and plunge, reinforces the feeling of a vastness in nature impossible to experience from a single, fixed viewpoint.

International Art

The Gallery's international collection spans the period from the fourteenth century to the present. Including paintings, prints, drawings, sculpture and decorative arts, the works have been acquired since the Gallery's inception and tell us much about the changing ways in which Australians have viewed their public collections. Works acquired in the Gallery's formative years were predominantly European, British artists being particularly well represented. More recent acquisitions however, reflect not only the major art movements of Europe and the United States, but also contemporary Australia's regional concerns, with works from the Asia-Pacific area becoming an important collection focus. The international collection provides visitors with the opportunity of viewing a number of significant works from historical and contemporary art movements, and plays an important role in contextualising Australian art practices since European settlement.

The works which formed the nucleus of the international collection in 1895 were, as with the Australian collections, acquired through donation. They include a group of Dutch seventeenth-century paintings of still lifes, landscapes and religious images by Jan Brueghel the Younger, Alexander Coosemans, Cornelis de Briers, Pieter van der Velde and after David Teniers the Younger, the bequest of the Hon. T.L. Murray-Prior.

The Gallery's first purchase (in 1896) was British artist Blandford Fletcher's *Evicted* 1887, the sentimental treatment of the subject-matter being reflective of late Victorian tastes in narrative painting. *Evicted* set the tone for other early acquisitions. The bonds of Empire then being strong, works by nineteenth-century British artists predominated. By the early years of the twentieth century, the Gallery had acquired a number of nineteenth- century works, including Frederick Goodall's *The Holy Mother* 1875, Henry Hewitt's *Season of mists and mellow fruitfulness* 1893, Hamilton Macallum's *Sunday afternoon parade* 1896 and

Philip Calderon's *Elizabeth Woodville, widow of Edward IV, parting with her younger son, the Duke of York* 1893, many of which were purchased after display at the Royal Academy's annual exhibitions in London. Also acquired at this time was *The deserted Costanza* c.1783–84, an important eighteenth-century painting by Angelica Kauffman, a founder of the Royal Academy.

This vitality in collecting activity was shortlived, however. Despite agitation in Brisbane for an expanded Gallery facility, a representative in London to assist in the acqusition of works and appeals made in the British press for donations of works, Government support for the Gallery waned. By 1932 a survey of Australian museums and galleries judged the Queensland Art Gallery to have 'the smallest income of any national art gallery in the British Empire'. During the ensuing years collecting became sporadic, with only a few significant acquisitions being made for the international collection.

In the 1950s, with the appointment of Robert Haines as Director, acquisition for the Gallery's international collection gained new momentum and direction, focusing on nineteenth and early twentieth-century European artists. A generous donation of funds from Major Harold de Vahl Rubin made possible the purchase of seven works including Picasso's *La Belle Hollandaise* 1905, still considered the Gallery's masterwork. Also included in the purchase were two Picasso drawings, Renoir's *Coco et Jean* c.1904–05, Vlaminck's *Still life*, Toulouse-Lautrec's *Tête de fille (Head of a girl)* 1892, and Degas's *Trois danseuses à la classe de dance* c.1888–90, ensuring the beginnings of a small but important modern European collection.

This acquisition of French works was complemented by the addition of a selection of late nineteenth-century French bronzes, including Edgar Degas's *The dancer* cast c.1919–21 and *Study for portrait of Madame S* cast c.1919–21; Auguste Rodin's *L'Age du bronze (Age of bronze)*, *La Femme accroupie (Crouching woman)* and *L'Acrobate (The acrobat)*; and Renoir's *Madame Renoir* c.1916. In later years these were augmented by etchings and lithographs of the period, including those by Charles Meryon, Pierre Bonnard and other members of the Nabis; Paul Cézanne; and Paul Gauguin.

Important British works were also acquired. These included portraits by Thomas Gainsborough and John Opie, and *Aurora* 1896 by the Pre-Raphaelite artist Edward Burne-Jones. The modern period became well represented with bronzes by Jacob Epstein and Elisabeth Frink, and works by Walter Richard Sickert, Walter Greaves, Philip Wilson Steer, Roger Fry, Duncan Grant, Spencer Gore, Stanley Spencer, Matthew Smith, Bernard Meninsky and Augustus John.

The decorative arts collection, initiated in the Haines era, depended largely on the support of donors, but it was not until the 1970s that significant acquisitions were made. The bequest of Mrs Blanche Buttner in 1972 included a fine chinoiserie table and the bequest of Dr Ernest Singer in 1975 included a significant collection of Bohemian glass. In the 1990s the gifts of Mr and Mrs J.W. Ellis added substantially to the English porcelain collection. The decorative arts items complement the Gallery's international works in other media, although international art glass since 1880 is a special focus collection.

A significant addition was made to the collection in 1965 when a wax relief by Giambologna was gifted by the Queensland Museum. This work was a study for one of six bronze panels designed by Giambologna for the doors of the Grimaldi Chapel in Genoa. Three wax reliefs from the series are also in the collection of the Victoria and Albert Museum in London.

The intended move to the Gallery's new premises on the south bank of the Brisbane River in 1982 prompted renewed interest in and attention to the collection of international works. From the 1970s, the Gallery benefited from the generosity of Lady Trout, who gifted numerous works to both the Australian and international collections from the collection of Sir Leon and Lady Trout, including a major

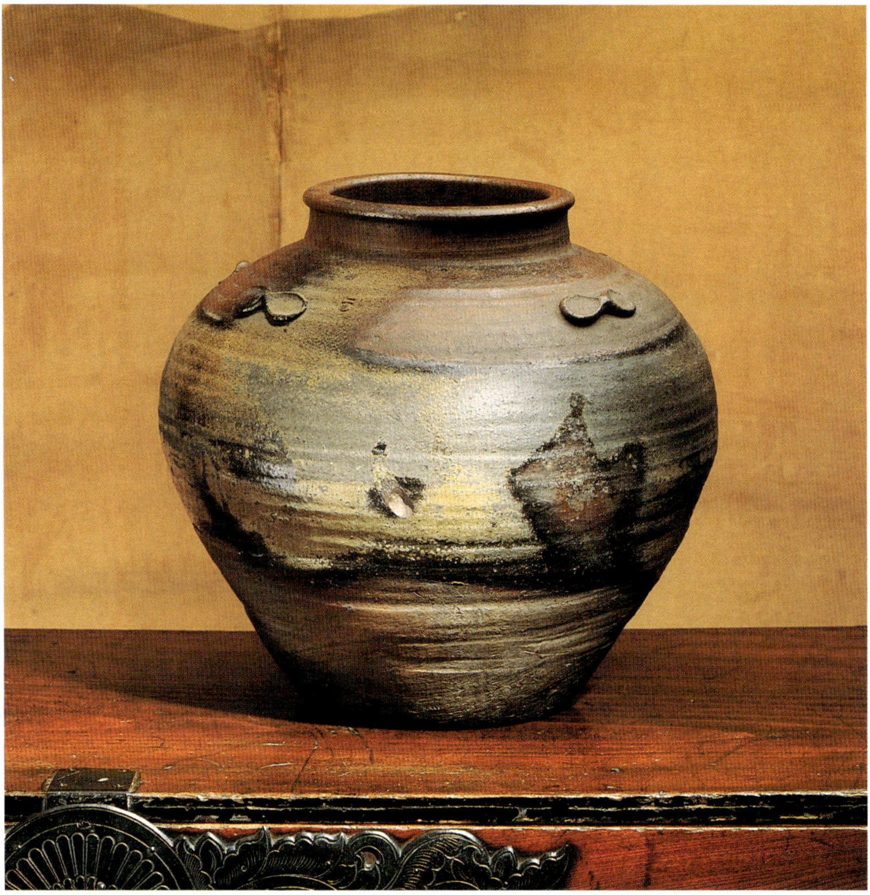

Bizen Kilns
Japan
Narrow-necked jar with lugs (tsubo) c.1574–1602
(Momoyama period)
Stoneware, coil built with natural ash glaze
30.9 x 35cm (diam.)
Purchased 1994 with funds from Idemitsu Kosan Co., Ltd through the Queensland Art Gallery Foundation

During the medieval period the Bizen potteries produced typical wares such as tsubo (jars), kame (wide-mouthed jars) and suribachi (grating dishes). The Bizen kilns were fired six or seven times a year, a process which could take up to forty days and which demanded the cooperation of the community. Chinese-inspired tea-storage jars featuring four raised loops on the shoulder, such as this example, were also produced from the fifteenth century. This jar is credited with being one of the most beautiful of the Momoyama period.

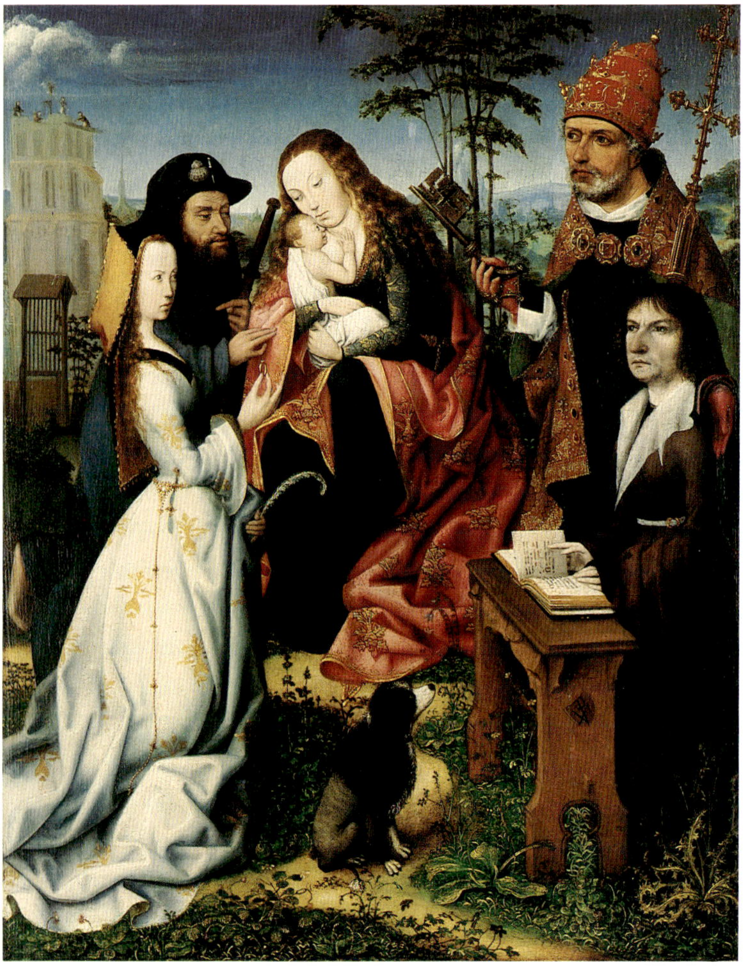

The Master of Frankfurt
The Netherlands
1460–c.1520–33
Virgin and Child with Saint James the Pilgrim, Saint Catherine and the Donor with Saint Peter c.1496
Oil on panel
70.4 x 56.2cm
Purchased 1980 with funds presented by the Utah Foundation through the Queensland Art Gallery Foundation

This panel is typical of fifteenth-century Netherlandish painting in its religious subject-matter and symbolic themes. It was commissioned by a wealthy man whose image is shown at the right kneeling at a prayer desk, his head superimposed over that of a female Donor, whose feminine body, clothing and hands are still visible. The painting would originally have hung in a church, and the rich symbolism and identity of the figures would have been readily understood by its intended audience.

portrait by the eighteenth-century British artist George Romney. A sizeable group of British artists prints of the 1960s and 1970s (lithographs from the Curwen Studio and screenprints from Kelpra Studio) was acquired in the late 1970s and early 1980s.

With the support of the newly established Queensland Art Gallery Foundation, an ambitious program of purchases was undertaken from 1980 by Director Raoul Mellish. The first work purchased through the Foundation was a late fifteenth-century panel by The Master of Frankfurt, *Virgin and Child with Saint James the Pilgrim, Saint Catherine and the Donor with Saint Peter* c.1496. This acquisition was quickly followed by Van Dyck's *Portrait of Marchese Filippo Spinola* c.1622–27, Tintoretto's *The Risen Christ (Cristo Risorgente)* c.1550, Rubens's *Young woman in a fur wrap* c.1629–30, Vuillard's *Le Salon des Hessel* c.1906, Sonia Delaunay's tapestry *Syncopée* c.1973–74, Moholy-Nagy's *Prehistoric construction* 1942, a drawing by Boucher and bronzes by Foggini, Carpeaux and Gauguin. Significant prints by Picasso, Rouault, Bonnard, Redon, Gauguin, Vuillard and Fantin-Latour were also purchased.

The momentum of significant purchases and donations continued after the opening of the new Gallery. Over the next few years acquisitions ranged from works by Old Masters, such as a panel fragment attributed to Lucas Cranach the Elder and a portrait by Cornelius Jonson, to modern and contemporary works from Europe and the United States by Léger, Giacometti, Kandinsky, Cézanne, Matisse, de Kooning, Dubuffet, Riley, Appel, Marini, Lipchitz, Miro, Paladino and Caro. Mimmo Paladino's *Canto notturno* 1984 is a commanding bronze purchased a year after production, and Bridget Riley's painting *Big blue* 1981 is arguably the most impressive work by the artist in an Australian collection.

Subsequently, under the direction of Doug Hall, the Gallery's international collection developed in new areas. Notable purchases included Leon Dudreville's *Expansion of poetry* 1913 (the earliest abstract painting in an Australian public collection); an early surrealist work by Yves Tanguy *Dung on the left, violets on the right (Fumier à gauche, violettes à droite)*; Chaim Soutine's expressionist painting *Man with ribbons (L'homme aux rubans)* 1921–22; Richard Long's installation *Ring of stones* 1982; and a commanding contemporary German expressionist painting by George Baselitz, *Im wald (In the forest)* 1990. The large group of Fluxus multiples donated by Francesco Conz in 1995 is significant for Australian collections. Since 1991 the funds generated by the Gallery's International Exhibitions Program have been an important source for acquisitions and reflect the developing entrepreneurial role of the Gallery.

Probably the most exciting new collecting activity centred on works from the Asia-Pacific region. In the 1990s, acquisitions of ceramics from the Six Old Kilns of Japan, initiated by the then Chairman of Trustees, Richard Austin, added to the Asian works that have entered the Gallery's collection over the years, generally as gifts from specialist collectors. These include *Ukiyo*-e prints, notably those gifted by the late Professor Joyce Ackroyd (who also donated a collection of *netsuke* and *inro*), and a pair of *Toeki* screens gifted by Mr James O. Fairfax, AO. Many of these works are displayed in the Gallery's ARCO Gallery of Asian Art.

The inaugural Asia-Pacific Triennial of Contemporary Art held in 1993 marked the beginning of a strong focus on contemporary art of the region. While contemporary prints, drawings and photographs from the Asia-Pacific area, particularly Japan, have been acquired over a number of years, the Triennial has encouraged the Gallery to expand its holdings to reflect the practice of art in all media in the region. This has been aided by the establishment of the Kenneth and Yasuko Myer Collection of Contemporary Asian Art, which includes works by artists from south-east and east Asia such as Heri Dono, Sulaiman Esa, Montien Boonma, Nguyen Xuan Tiep, Vasan Sitthiket, Dadang Christanto, Dede Eri Supria and Shigeo Toya. Xu Bing's *A book from the sky* 1987–91 is an outstanding acquisition in this regard.

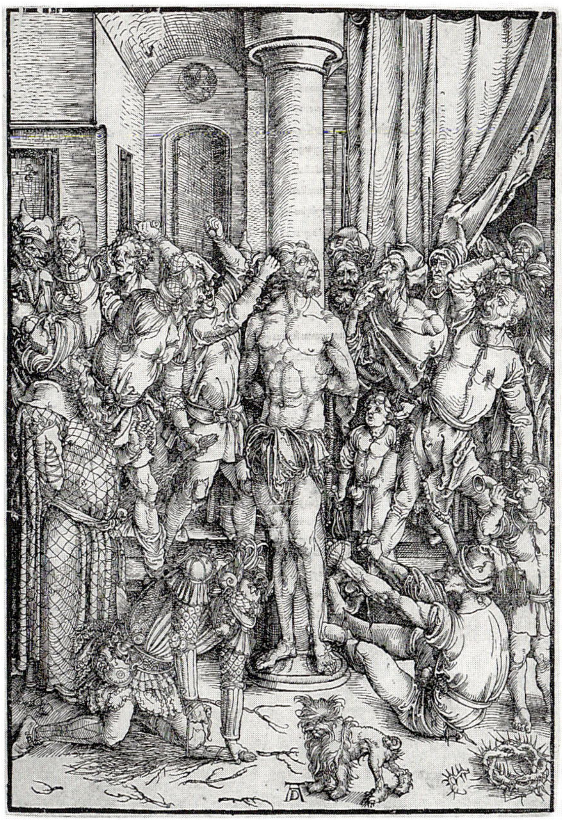

Albrecht Dürer
Germany 1471–1528
***The flagellation of Christ* (from 'The Large Passion')** c.1496–97
Woodcut
38.6 x 27.3cm (comp.)
Gift of Mrs Selina Rivers 1949

Two of Dürer's most famous series of woodblock prints, published with Latin text in 1511, are the 'Apocalypse' (fifteen cuts) and 'The Large Passion' (twelve cuts). In spite of their traditional subjects, they are revolutionary in scale and subtlety of technique. They show Dürer's discovery of Renaissance ideas of three-dimensionality. His art still had all the power of the Gothic—elongated gaunt figures and sinewy lines—but in emulation of pen and ink drawings, Dürer's lines taper or swell to give variations of light and shade not seen before in the production of woodcuts.

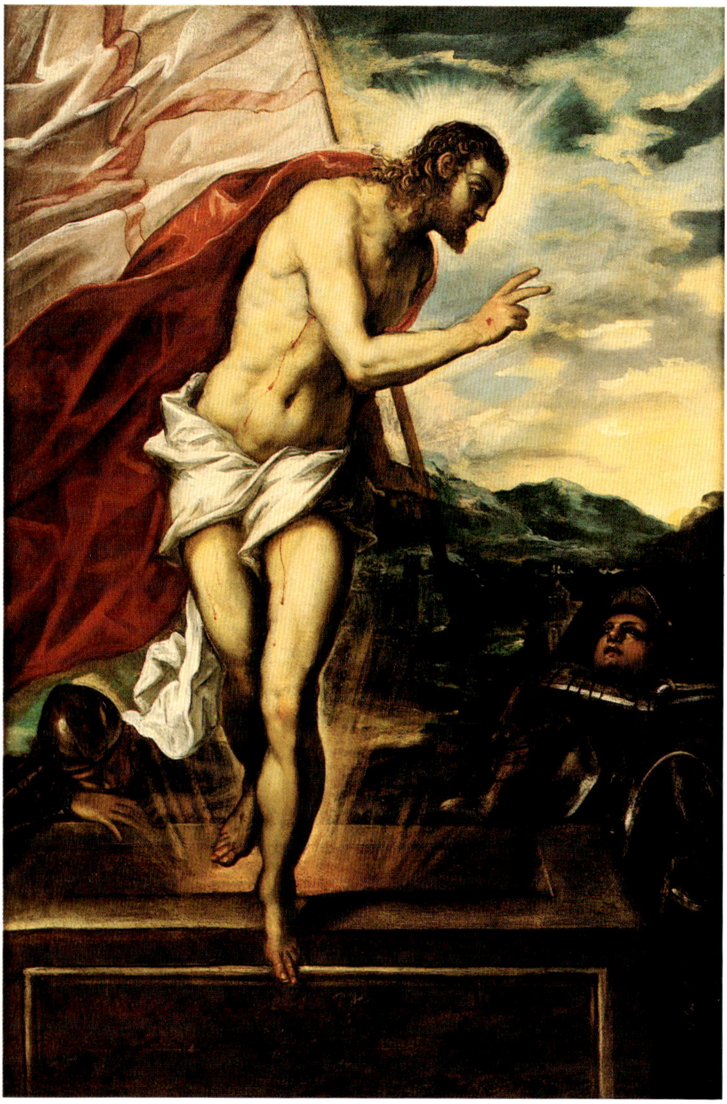

Tintoretto
Venice 1518–94
The Risen Christ (Cristo Risorgente) c.1550
Oil on canvas
201 x 139cm
Purchased 1981. Queensland Art Gallery Foundation

Tintoretto is widely acknowledged as one of the Masters of the Venetian Renaissance. His rapidly executed canvases display a powerful, even theatrical vitality. This version of The Risen Christ *is thought to be the third on the subject painted by the artist and represents a bold advance on the two previous works. In its original church setting (probably as an altarpiece) placed high above the spectator, the dramatic illusionism of the foreshortened figure of Christ would have been more pronounced.*

To contextualise the later twentieth-century works, the Gallery has made a commitment to acquire works by significant earlier twentieth-century Asian artists. *Self portrait in Kusamba Beach* 1983 by Affandi, generally acknowledged as one of Indonesia's greatest artists, is the first of these acquisitions.

Since its inception in 1895, the Gallery has accrued a small but significant group of international art works in a program of collecting activity that is reflective of Queensland's changing cultural environment and the vision of a number of influential individuals. From the initial group of predominantly British works, the Gallery's international collection has expanded to include works from all over Europe, the United States and more recently Asia, developing into a diverse and intellectually challenging State collection.

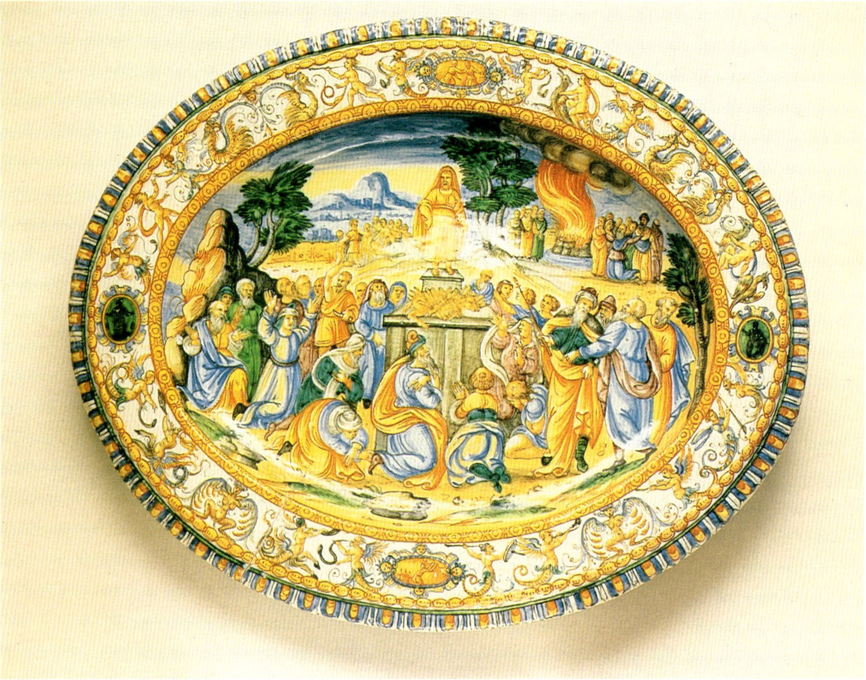

Conrade Frères (Nevers)
France 1588–c.1680
Majolica platter (The Prophet Elijah confronting the priests of Baal on Mount Carmel) c.1600–18
Earthenware
6.5 x 62 x 50cm
Purchased 1993

The Nevers majolica works were among the earliest in France and produced 'istoriato' (literally 'story painted') wares imitating those of contemporary Italy. The biblical story depicted here reflects the period of conflict between Catholic and Protestant (Les Guerres de Religion 1570–96) which ended during the reign of Henry of Navarre. His second marriage to Marie de Medici produced a son in 1601 — the first Dauphin (Crown Prince) born to the throne of France in nearly six decades. Dolphins — the French word is 'dauphin' — decorate the obverse in recognition of this event.

Right
Cornelius Jonson
England/The Netherlands
1593–1661
Portrait of a lady c.1640
Oil on canvas
82.7 x 64.8cm
Purchased 1983. Queensland Art Gallery Foundation, with funds donated in memory of J. B. Reid

Cornelius Jonson was born in London of Dutch parents and is considered to be among the first portraitists to create works that are wholly British in character. Jonson's most obvious qualities are his sensitivity to the personality of his sitter and his feeling for the domestic portrait. His work is characterised by a meticulously detailed draftsmanship and elegant style that may indicate some training in miniatures. Portrait of a lady *represents his mature period.*

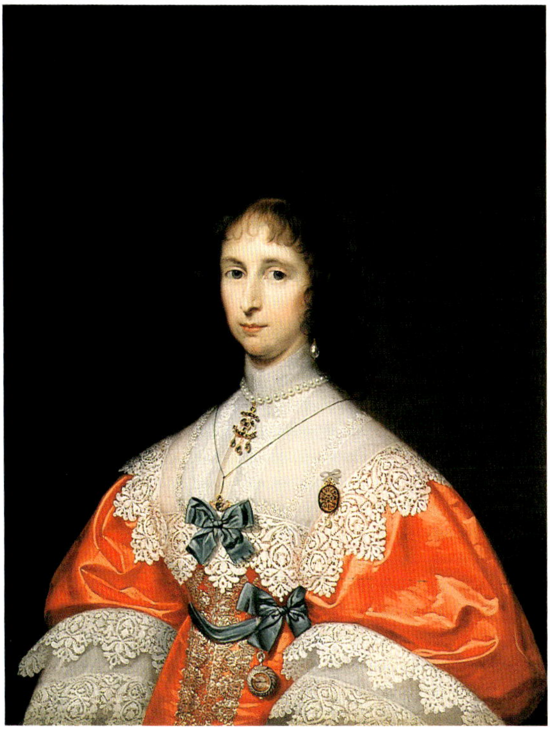

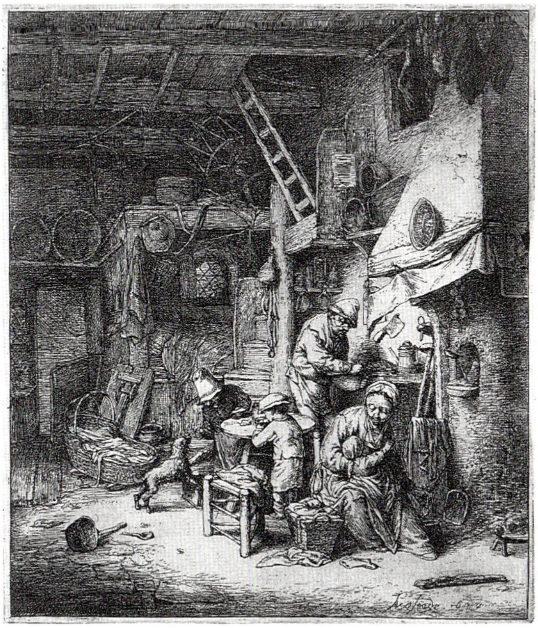

Left
Adriaen van Ostade
The Netherlands 1610–85
The family 1647
Etching
17.7 x 15.8cm (comp.)
Purchased 1989. Queensland Art Gallery Foundation

Representation of the everyday life of the peasantry was the chief theme of Haarlem-based artist Adriaen van Ostade. Intimate scenes of families preparing meals, or taverns with boisterous drinking and dancing, were the subject of many of his paintings and etchings. He was the leading exponent of genre scenes, which are readily identified with seventeenth-century Netherlandish art. Van Ostade's vigorous line etchings (approximately fifty) belong to the years 1647–71, the earliest of which show him at his strongest.

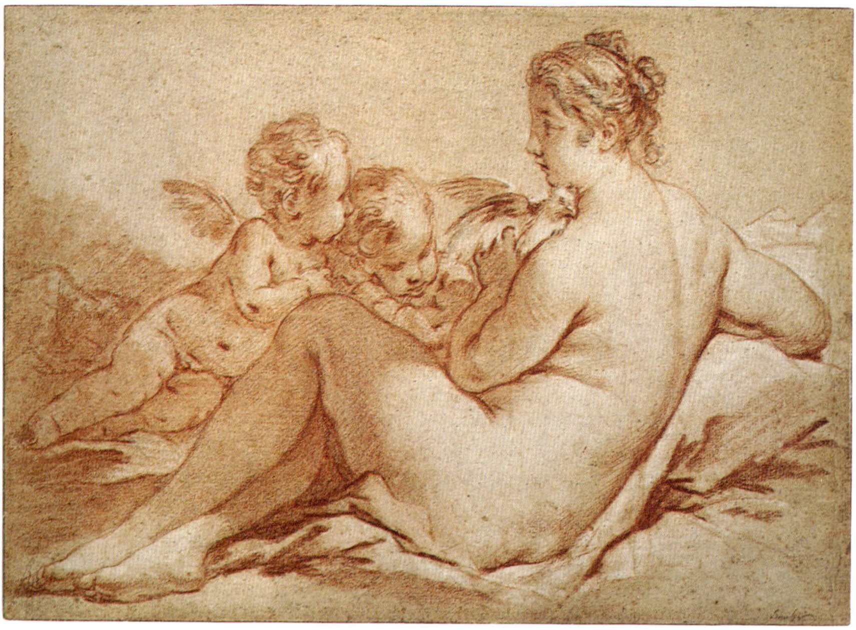

François Boucher
France 1703–70
Venus with two cherubs (Vénus avec deux angelots) c.1740
Chalk
25 x 35.9cm
Purchased 1978

Boucher was director of the Gobelins tapestry workshop before being appointed 'King's Painter' to Louis XV of France. He mastered all forms of decorative painting from palace interiors to stage designs and fans. His style epitomises the playful and elegant style of the French court in the mid eighteenth century. This sanguine (red chalk) drawing is a study for the oil Birth of Venus *1743 and was formerly in the Alfred de Rothschild Collection.*

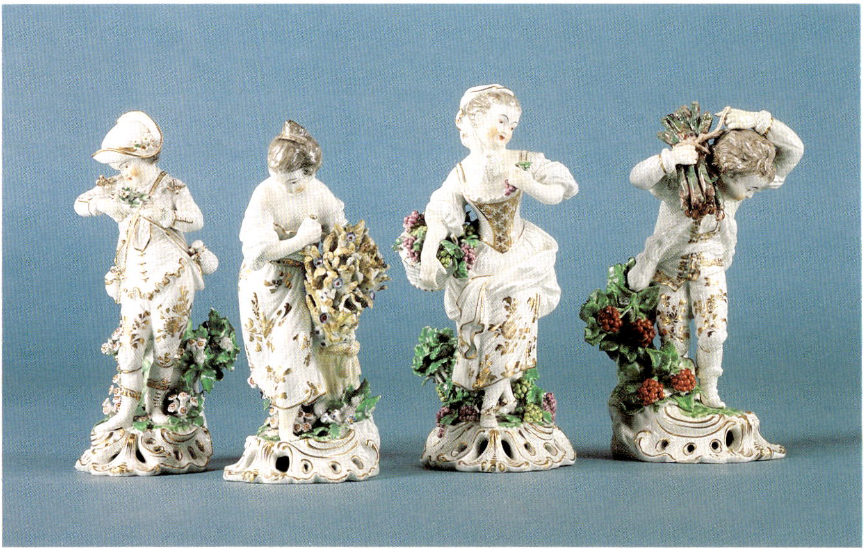

Chelsea Porcelain Works
(Chelsea-Derby)
England 1769–84
François Boucher
France 1703–70
Pierre Stephan
England unknown
Figurines: The French seasons c.1775–80
Porcelain, polychrome and gilt
17.9cm (max. ht)
Gift of Mr J. W. Ellis in memory of Charles and Beatrice Cossart, Boonah 1994

In the experimental years of European porcelain manufacturing, there was much interchange of formulae and designs between the various factories. François Boucher, court painter to Louis XV, was a master of decorative painting and provided designs for Beauvais tapestries and Sèvres porcelain. His design 'The four seasons' became the source for a group of models made by Nicolas Gauron for the porcelain works at Tournai. Gauron and another modeller, Pierre Stephan, went to work at the Chelsea Factory in London about 1771, so it is not surprising that this delightful set of figures, entitled The French seasons*, parallel those produced at Tournai.*

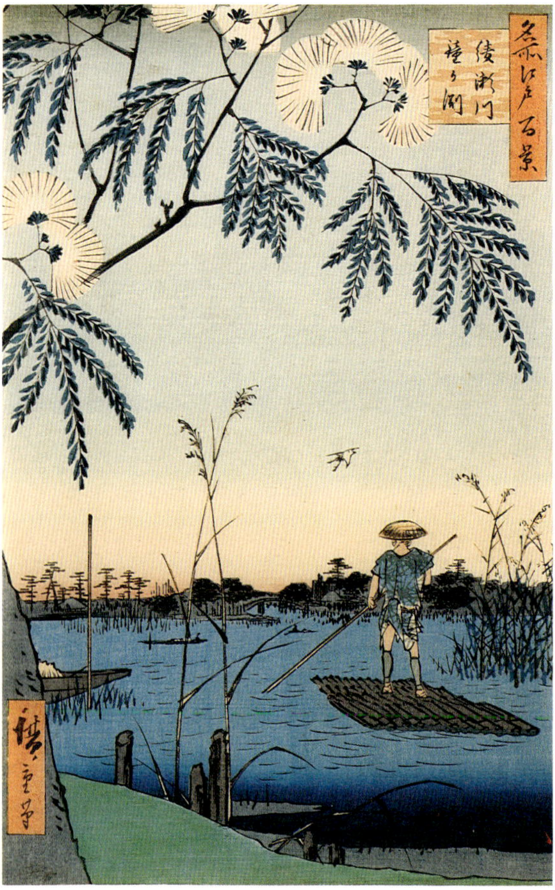

Ichiryusai Hiroshige
Japan 1797–1858
***Ayase-gawa, kane-ga-guchi* (no.69 from the 'One hundred famous views of Edo' series)** 1857
Colour woodblock print
33 x 21.5cm
Purchased 1992. Queensland Art Gallery Foundation

The last master of the Ukiyo-e *school of woodblock printing, Hiroshige specialised in landscape, becoming the most acclaimed artist of this genre. Landscape prints came into vogue after travel restrictions were lifted in Japan in the 1820s and it became easier to travel within the country. This created a demand for mementos of journeys as well as a novelty for armchair travellers. 'Meisho Edo Hyakkei' ('One hundred views of Edo') actually comprised 119 prints.*

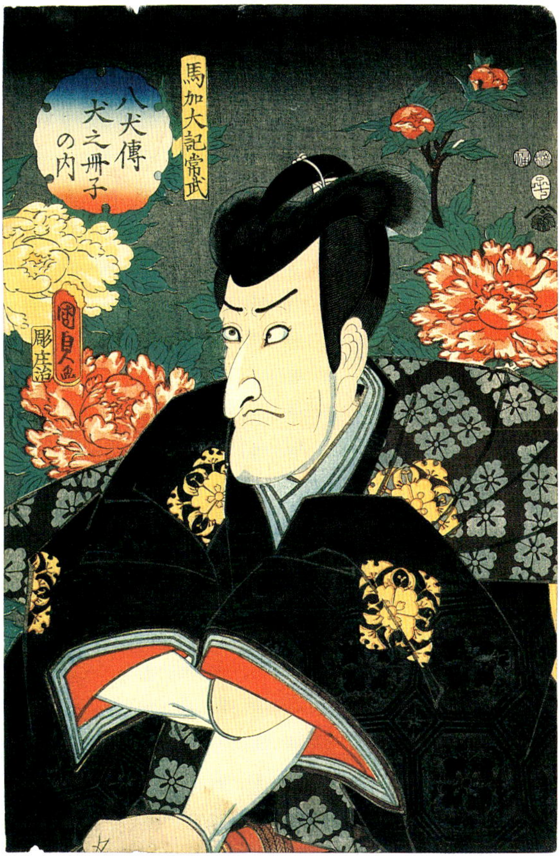

Kunisada II
Japan 1823–80
The samurai Makuwa Daiki Tsunetake from Bakkin's 'Hakkenden' 1852
Colour woodblock print
36×24.5cm
Purchased 1976

The colour woodblock print emerged as a popular art form in Japan in the late seventeenth century, generated by the predominantly middle-class society which emerged with the new city of Edo (Tokyo). Ukiyo-e prints became known as 'pictures of the floating world' and recorded the passing events of daily life, the world of courtesans in their splendid kimonos, medieval heroic legends and the popular kabuki theatre. Kunisada II took his name from a leading Ukiyo-e artist and specialised in portraits of actors. The flat decorative colour, vital line and beautiful patterning are characteristic of traditional woodblock prints.

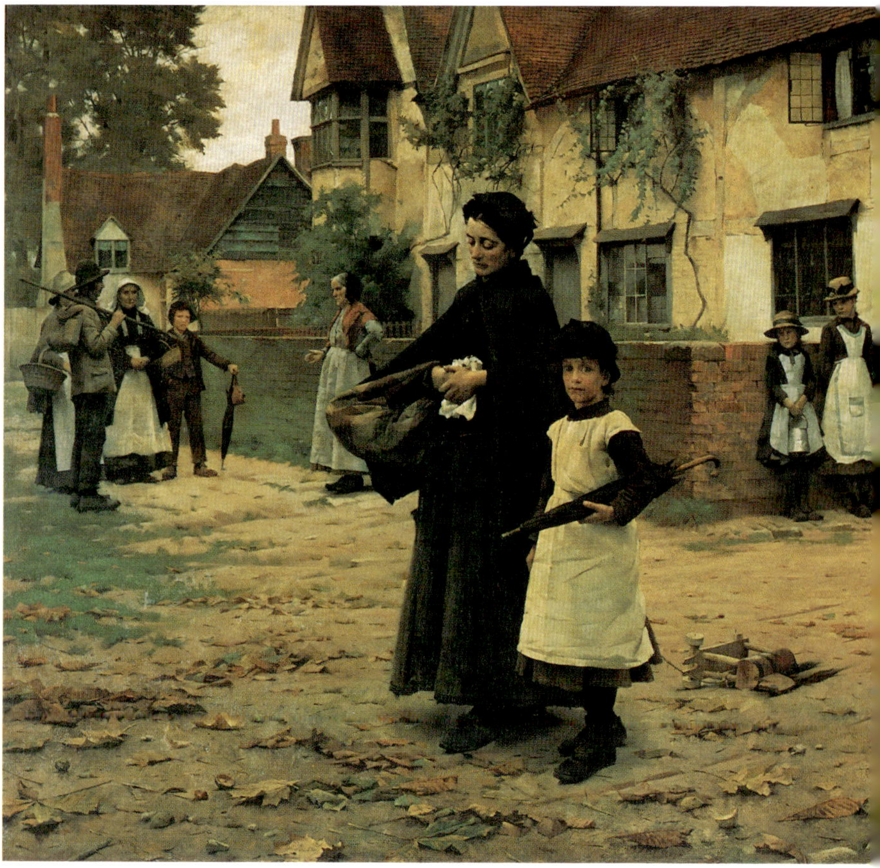

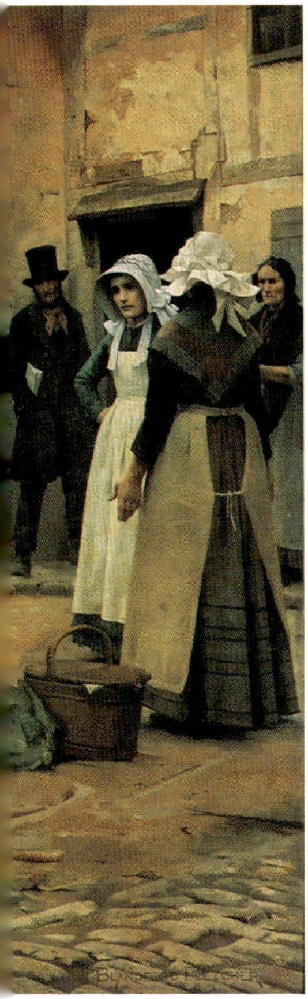

Blandford Fletcher
England 1858–1936
Evicted 1887
Oil on canvas
122.9 x 185.5cm
Purchased 1896

Blandford Fletcher was a member of the British Newlyn school, which was heavily influenced by the French pleinairists. English village life was his most frequent subject-matter and his treatment of it was typical of late Victorian, social realism style. Evicted *presents its narrative of a dispossessed widow and her child with pathos and a closely observed characterisation that elicits a sympathetic emotional response from the viewer.*
This painting was the first purchase of the newly founded Queensland National Art Gallery.

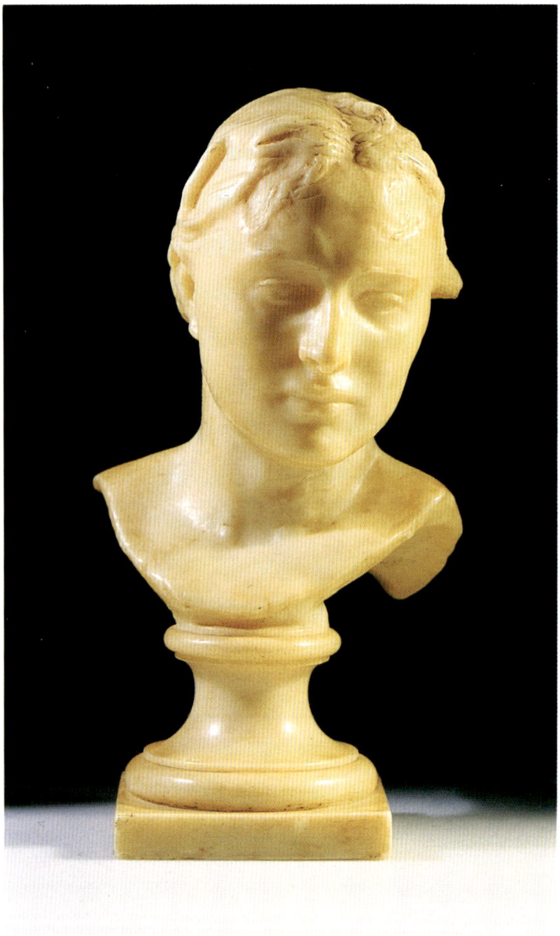

Auguste Rodin
France 1840–1917
Madame Russell 1888
Wax
33.2 x 27 x 24cm
Purchased 1992 with funds from the 1991 International Exhibitions Program

Rodin is regarded as one of the great figures in late nineteenth-century French art. His work, predominantly in bronze and marble, looked beyond neo-classical taste towards an expressionism that influenced the modernist sculptors of the early twentieth century. This wax bust is one of four made of the artist's model Marianna Mattiocco, who married expatriate Australian painter John Peter Russell. A friend of Rodin, Russell commissioned the bust, perhaps as a commemoration of his marriage in February 1888. Rodin considered Marianna to be the 'most beautiful woman in Paris' and commemorated her features in a number of subsequent works based on this bust.

Right
Henri de Toulouse-Lautrec
France 1864–1901
Divan Japonais 1892–93
Lithograph
79.6 x 60.2cm (comp.)
Purchased 1991

The Divan Japonais was a small cabaret in Paris, a café-concert for which Toulouse-Lautrec designed posters in the 1890s. Jane Avril, a famous cancan dancer, is depicted in the foreground with one of her admirers, the writer and critic Edouard Dujardin. Yvette Guilbert, the singer with her hallmark black gloves, performs on the stage. Toulouse-Lautrec is as highly regarded for his prints as for his paintings.

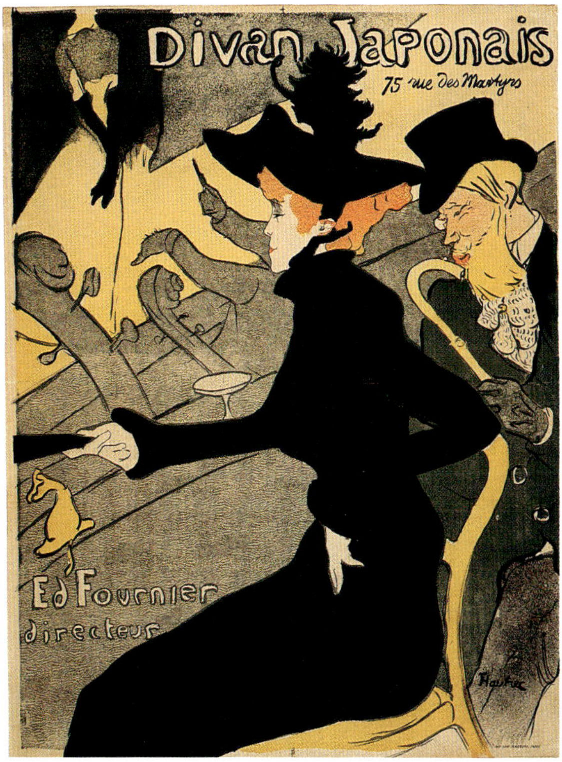

Below
Edgar Degas
France 1834–1917
Trois danseuses à la classe de danse (Three dancers at a dancing class) c.1888–90
Oil on cardboard
50.5 x 60.6cm
Purchased 1959 with funds donated by Major Harold de Vahl Rubin

Degas has been traditionally associated with the impressionists, who favoured new ways of recording 'modern' life. The rise of the bourgeoisie in nineteenth-century France led to the development of new leisure activities, and artists turned to the dance halls, theatres, racetracks, cafés, parks and boulevards for subject-matter. Working life was rarely portrayed, although Degas's images of laundresses, milliners and dancers were an exception. The ballet class motif is one used frequently by Degas, dancers comprising approximately half his subject-matter.

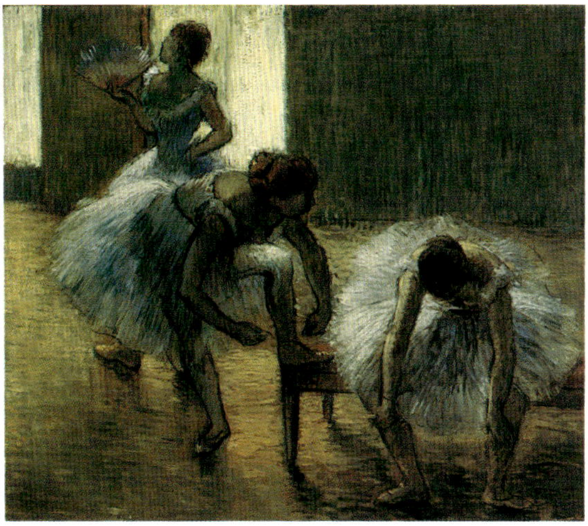

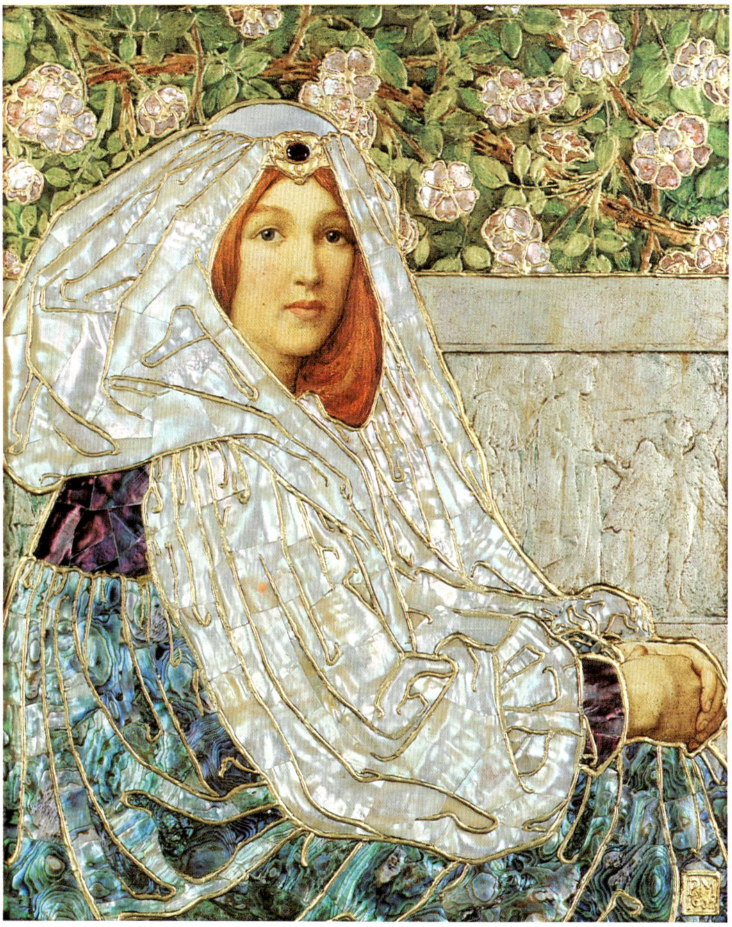

F.Pickford Marriott
England 1876–1935
Love in her eyes sits playing 1902
Gesso, oil, mother-of-pearl and semiprecious stones on wood panel
31.5 x 26.4cm
Purchased 1927

Pickford Marriott was born in England but grew up in Brisbane. He received his art education in both Brisbane and England, and in 1903 moved to South Africa where he taught at the Port Elizabeth School of Art. The various media in which Marriott worked were informed by the prevailing style of Pre-Raphaelism. He concentrated on allegorical themes and drew his inspiration from mythology and medieval legends. His romanticised escapism is exemplified in Love in her eyes sits playing, *which illustrates the medieval theme of the Virgin in the Rose Bower.*

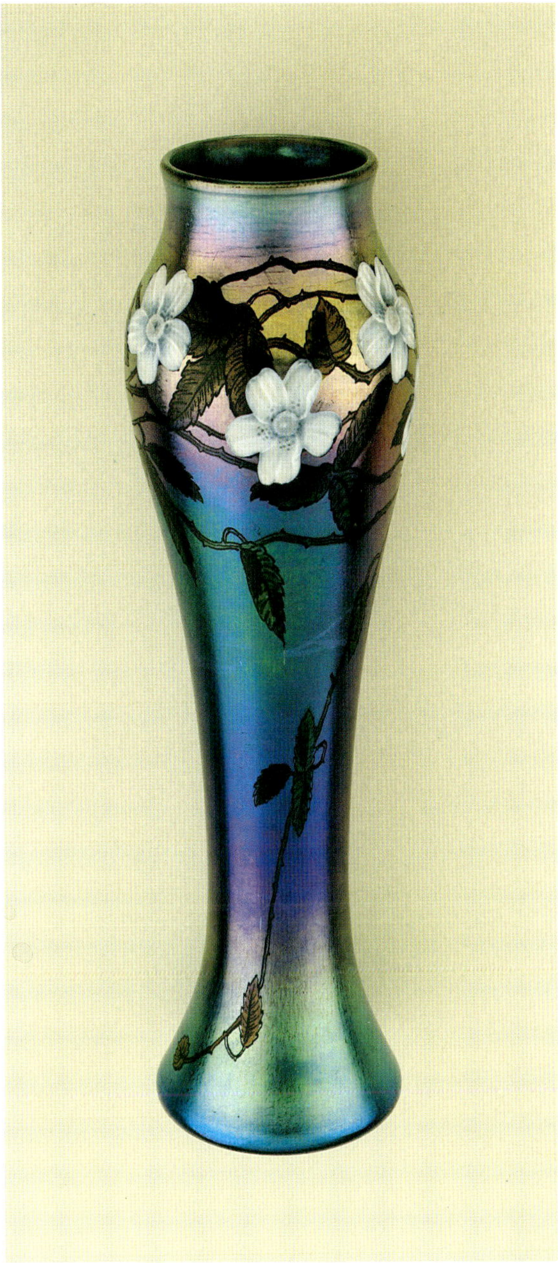

Louis Comfort Tiffany
United States 1848–1933
Baluster vase 1892–93
Iridescent glass padded and carved
38.5 x 9.5cm
Purchased 1983

Tiffany was the leading art nouveau designer in the United States. He initially began as an interior designer and became famous for his richly coloured, stained glass windows, but in 1892 established a successful commercial glass works. Following the 'truth to material' ethos of the Arts and Crafts movement, Tiffany used the fluidity of the glass to suggest movement or growth. His rich iridescent colours, achieved by fuming with metal salts in a kiln, were inspired by the degraded surface of ancient Roman glass.

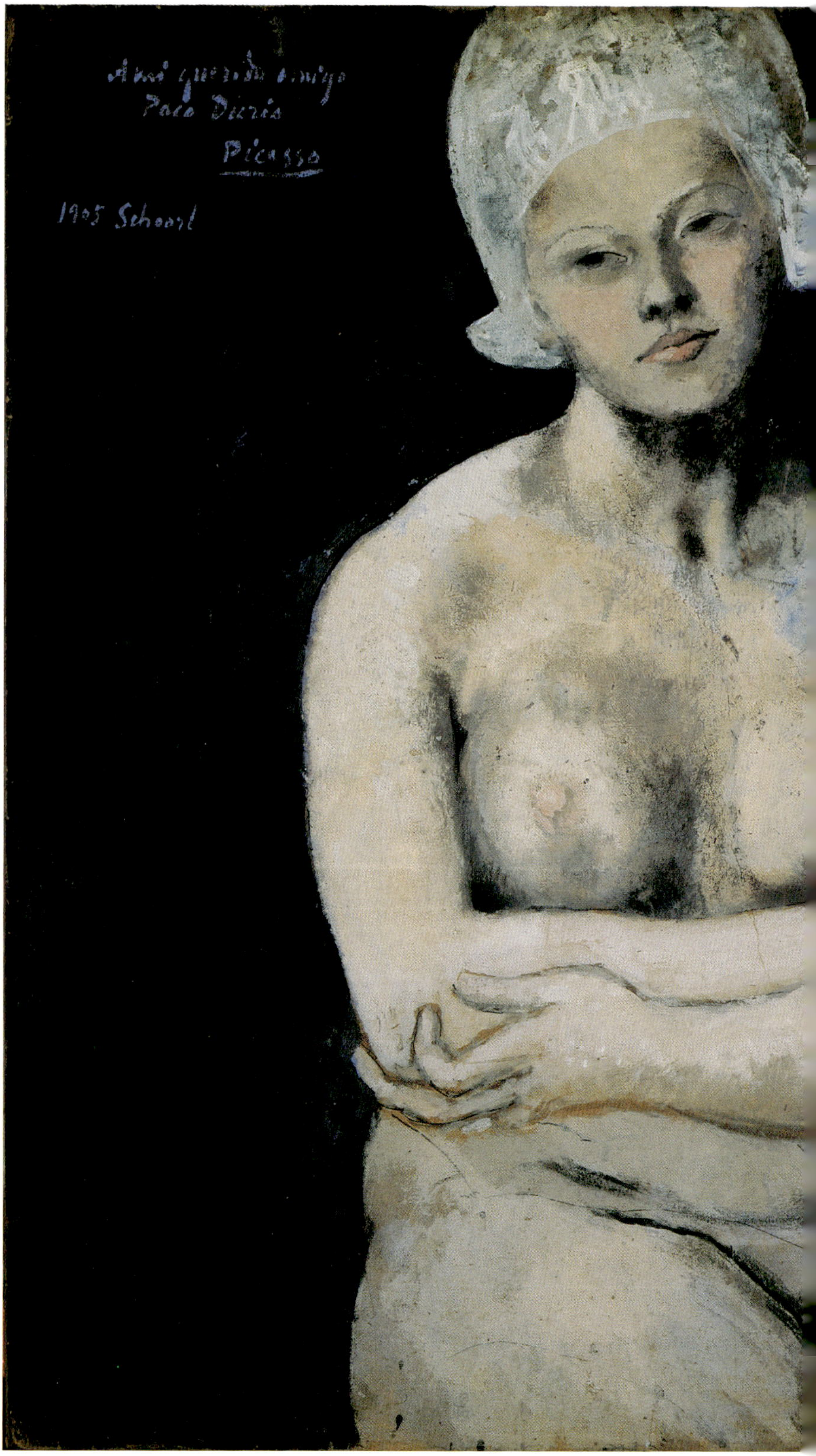
A mi querido amigo
Paco Durio
Picasso
1905 Schoorl

Pablo Picasso
Spain 1881–1973
La Belle Hollandaise 1905
Gouache on cardboard
77 x 66.3cm
Purchased 1959 with
funds donated by
Major Harold de Vahl Rubin

Over Picasso's long career, he achieved success of almost mythic proportions across a broad variety of media including painting, sculpture, drawing, printmaking and ceramics. La Belle Hollandaise *is an important transitional work from Picasso's early career between the starkness of the blue period and the gentler vein of the rose period. It was painted in the summer of 1905 when Picasso journeyed to the northern Netherlands, where he was struck by the statuesque appearance of Dutch women.* La Belle *. . . has a placidness and serenity which appears to prefigure Picasso's classical nudes of the 1920s.*

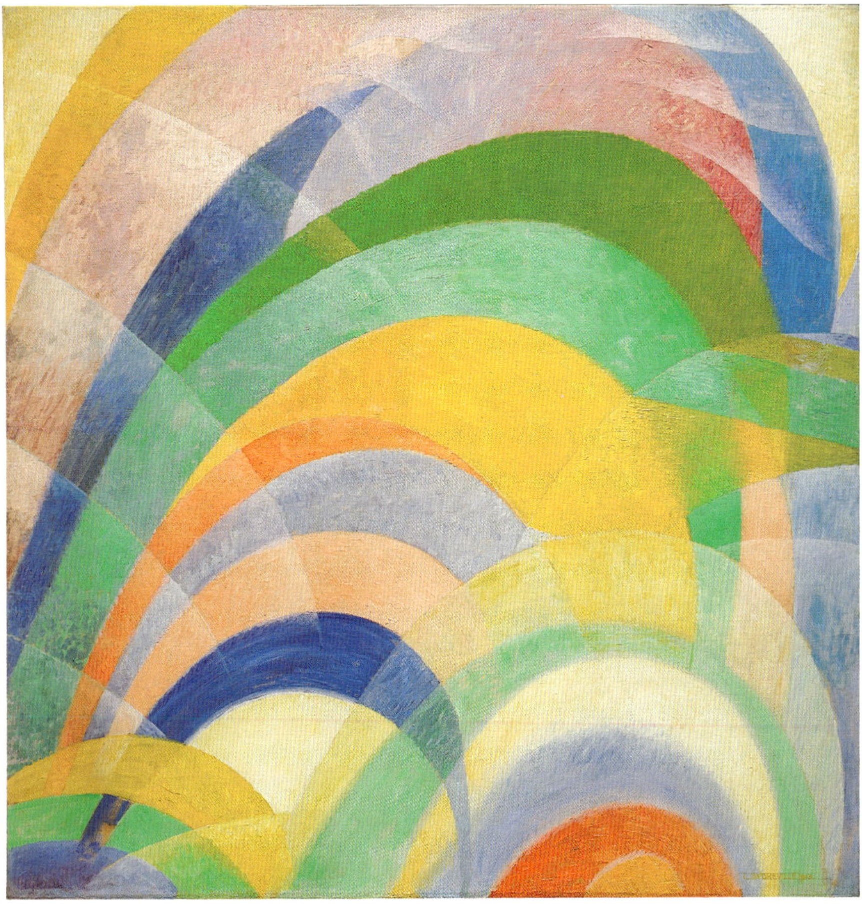

Leonardo Dudreville
Italy 1885–1975
Expansion of poetry 1913
Oil on canvas
129.5 x 129.5cm
Purchased 1994 with funds from the International Exhibitions Program

This work is an example of the radical Italian art movement known as futurism, founded by the poet Marinetti in 1908. Futurism sought to replace the existing cultural order with revolutionary models that celebrated modernity and technological advancement. This work explores the fusion of painting, poetry, and music. The radiating arcs of colour convey a sense of the dynamism and energy which was at the heart of the futurist philosophy. Expansion of poetry *is the earliest example of abstraction in an Australian public collection.*

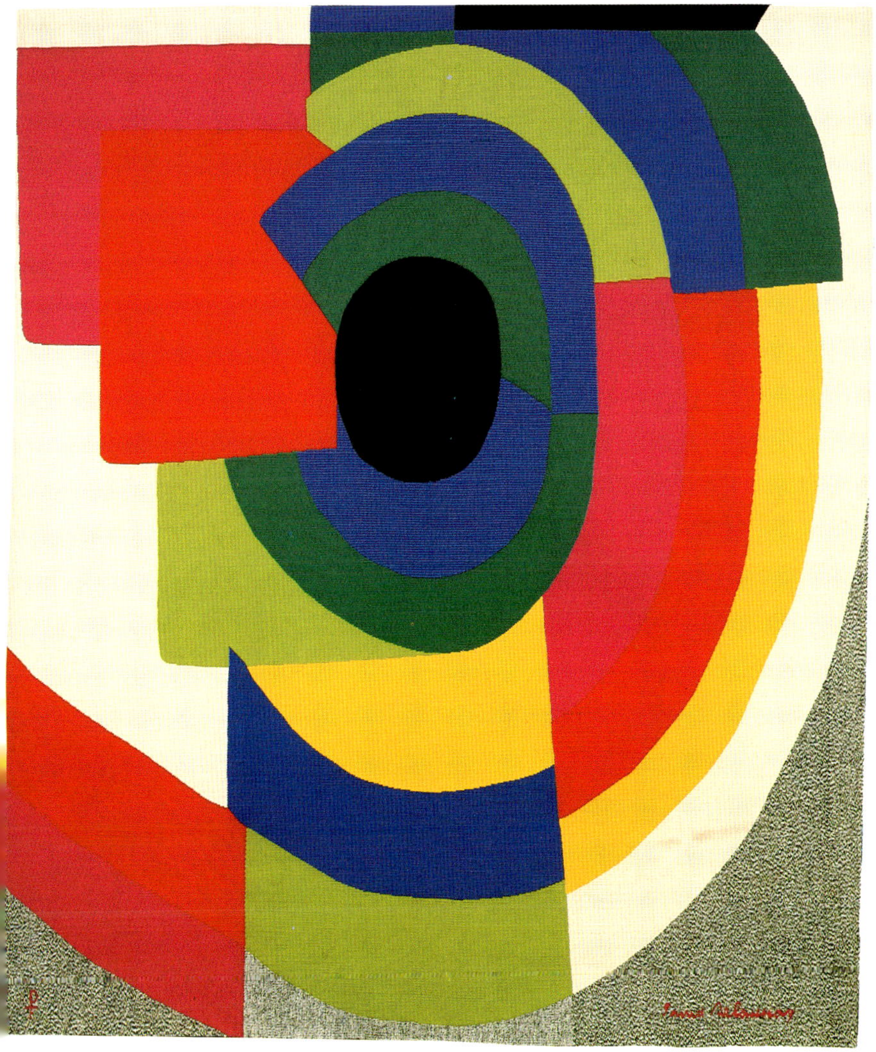

Sonia Delaunay
France 1885–1979
Pinton Atelier
France a.1970s
Tapestry: Syncopée
c.1973–74
Wool tapestry
ed. 4/6
200 × 175cm
Purchased 1980. Queensland Art Gallery Foundation with funds from the Queensland Art Gallery Society

Sonia Delaunay was the first woman artist honoured during her lifetime with an exhibition at the Louvre. She began her career in painting, but soon after meeting her husband, Robert, turned to decorative arts. Book illustrations, fashion design, furniture, interior design, and tapestries are only some of the areas in which she worked. The tapestry Syncopée *is typical of the dynamism of her work which focuses on the effects of colour and geometrical forms.*

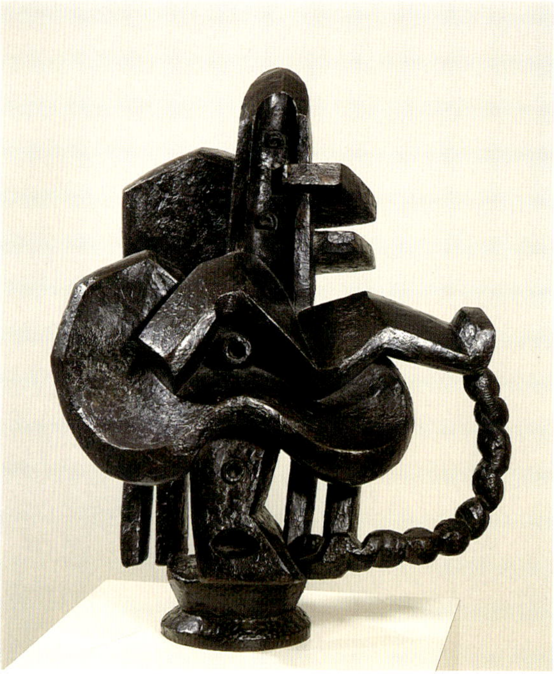

Left
Jacques Lipchitz
France/United States
1891–1973
Musical instruments 1925
(reworked at a later date)
Bronze
ed. 3/7
83 x 69.5 x 43 cm
Purchased 1983

Lipchitz is recognised as a leading exponent of cubist sculpture. Born in Lithuania, he went to France in 1909 where he befriended Picasso and Juan Gris, the founders of the cubist movement. In 1941 he fled from France to New York, where he worked for the remainder of his life. Musical instruments *was sculpted in Paris, although it was substantially reworked at a later date. It reflects the transition in Lipchitz's art from his earlier heavy, angular, synthetic cubist forms to an exploration of the spatial rather than solid qualities of sculpture.*

Right
Rowley Gallery
England 1898-unknown
Four fold screen c.1920–25
Inlaid and stained timber
Four screens: 189 x 35 cm (each)
Purchased 1988

This screen, composed in marquetry in a variety of stained timbers, was manufactured by the Rowley Gallery, London, which was established as an interior design company in 1898. The rhythmic patterns of the English landscape, with its villages and hedgerows, have been exaggerated here with stark dynamism and relate to contemporary printmaking at the Grosvenor School of Art or even the work of the vorticists.

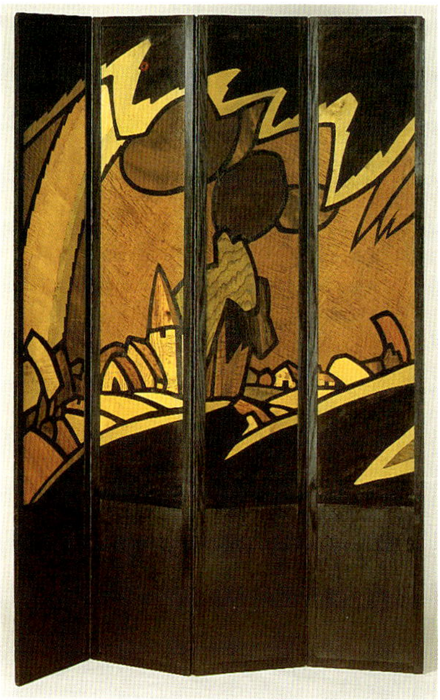

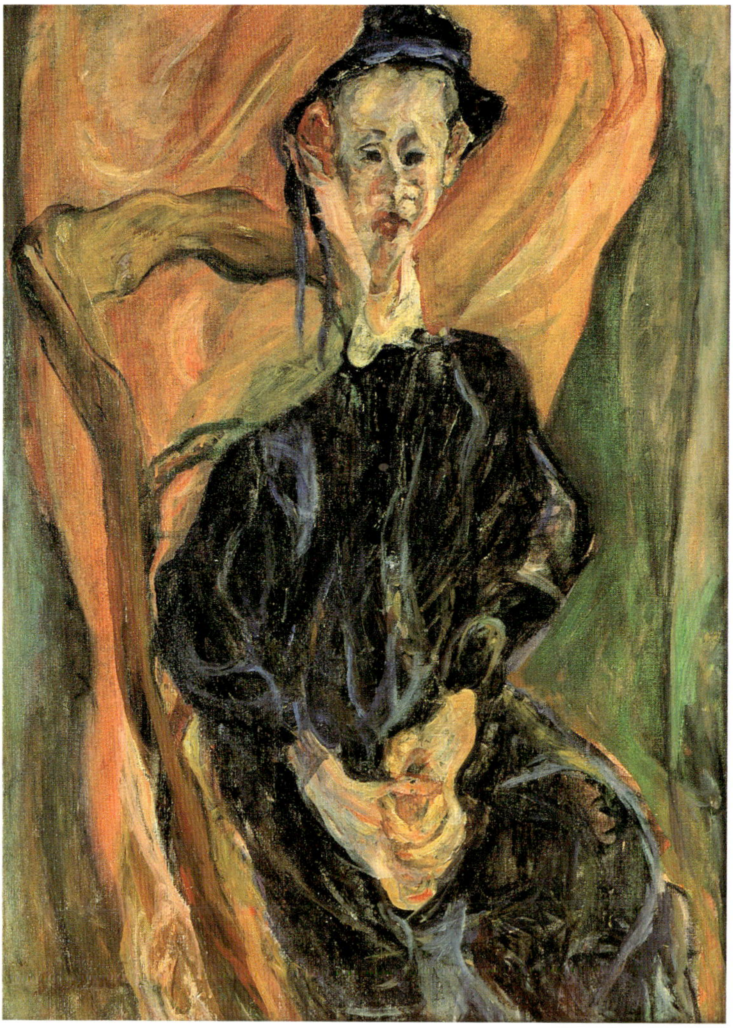

Chaim Soutine
France 1893–1943
Man with ribbons
(L'homme aux rubans)
1921–22
Oil on canvas
77.5 x 58.2cm
Purchased 1988 with funds from the 1988 International Exhibitions Program

Soutine produced highly original expressionist paintings that had a profound influence on later American abstract expressionists including Willem de Kooning. Originally from Lithuania, Soutine moved to Paris in 1913 where he became acquainted with Chagall, Lipchitz and Modigliani. From 1919 to 1922 Soutine lived in Céret in the Pyrenees, where his painting style matured and he produced some of his most significant works. Dating from this period, Man with ribbons *is almost abstract in its execution, combining a rhythmic flow of lines, distorted angles and raw colour.*

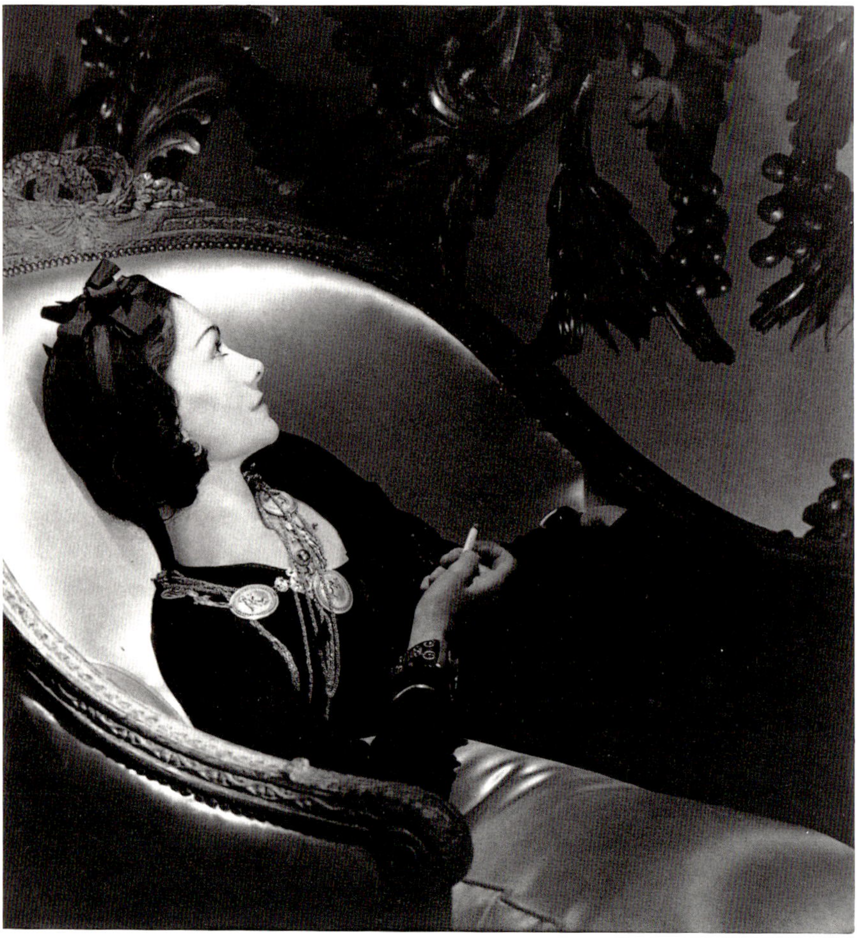

Horst P. Horst
Germany b.1906
Coco Chanel 1937
(printed 1982)
Gelatin silver photograph
18.2 x 17.4cm (comp.)
Purchased 1982

Chanel was one of the most celebrated fashion designers of the twentieth century. This portrait captures the qualities of luxurious fabrics, textures and surfaces, the heart of Chanel's success. From the 1930s, Horst worked as a fashion photographer for Vogue magazine, together with other luminaries of fashion photography such as Cecil Beaton and Irving Penn. Most of Horst's subjects were photographed indoors and his images have been lauded for their extraordinary lighting effects.

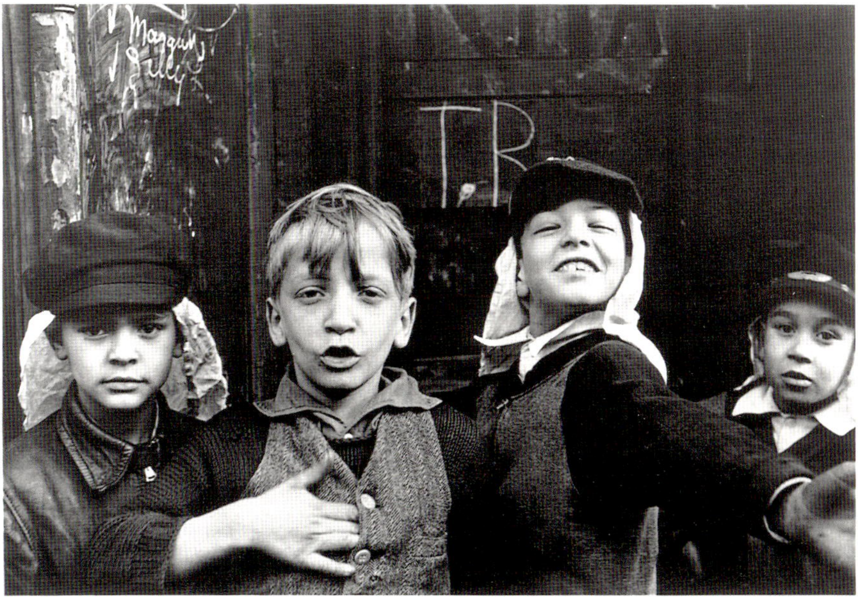

Helen Levitt
United States b.1918
(Untitled) c.1942
Gelatin silver photograph
16.2 x 24.2cm (comp.)
Purchased 1994 with funds from Joyce McCracken through the Queensland Art Gallery Foundation

Born in New York, Levitt often drew upon this city and its inhabitants as the subject of her photography. When she acquired a hand-held Leica camera in 1936, she was readily able to capture the telling gesture and movement of figures in the gritty urban environment. She moved in on her subjects, often capturing fleeting moments of childhood when one is least selfconscious and most extroverted. Untitled *shows four young boys who imitate imagined poses of French Foreign Legion soldiers and sport the distinctive 'kepi', fashioned out of their own caps and handkerchiefs.*

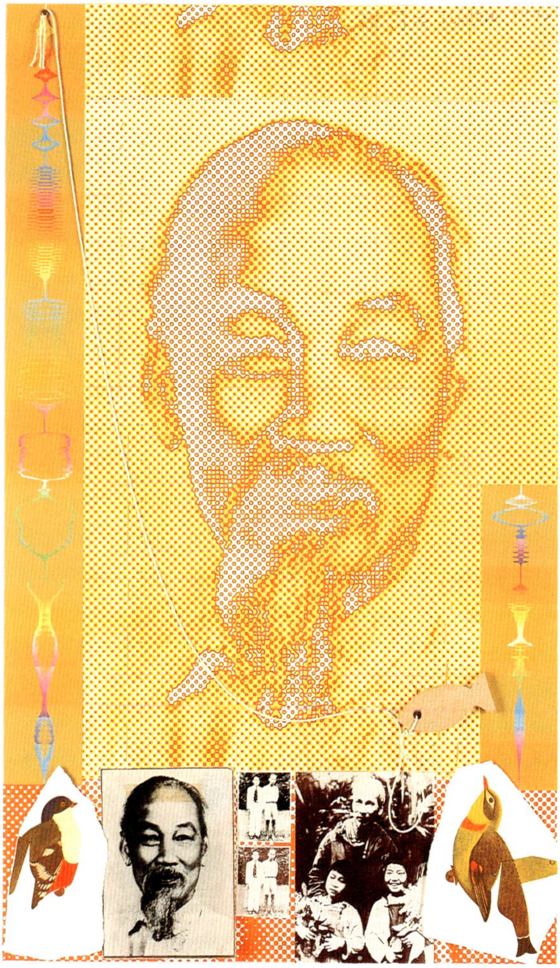

Joe Tilson
England b.1928
Ho Chi Minh 1970
Screenprint, photo-screenprint and collage
101 x 61 cm (comp.)
Purchased 1984

Tilson was one of the leading British artists of his generation, his prints achieving particular acclaim. Allied with the pop art movement in the 1960s, his work from this time presented complex themes, often producing an iconic quality. Ho Chi Minh *offers evidence of Tilson's interest in collage and multi-media combinations of materials. It was printed in collaboration with master printer Chris Prater at Kelpra Studio, London.*

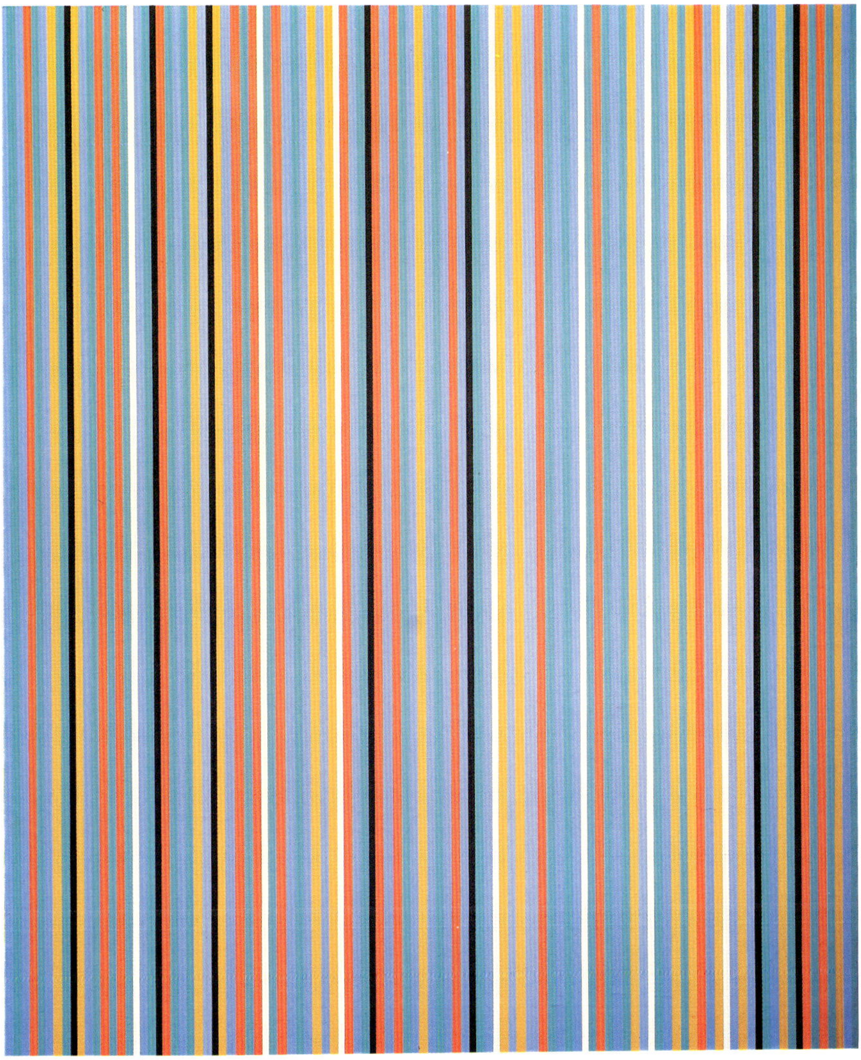

Bridget Riley
England b.1931
Big blue 1981
Oil on linen
234.5 x 201cm
Purchased 1984

Bridget Riley is often connected with the op art movement of the 1960s, although she objects to the connection and dismisses the movement as faddish. Op art refers to abstract works exploiting disruptive retinal effects through colour and shape. Riley is interested in exploring the potential of colour and its relationships. Big blue was painted after she visited Egypt in 1980–81, which had a profound effect upon her choice of palette, focusing it towards the brilliant Mediterranean light.

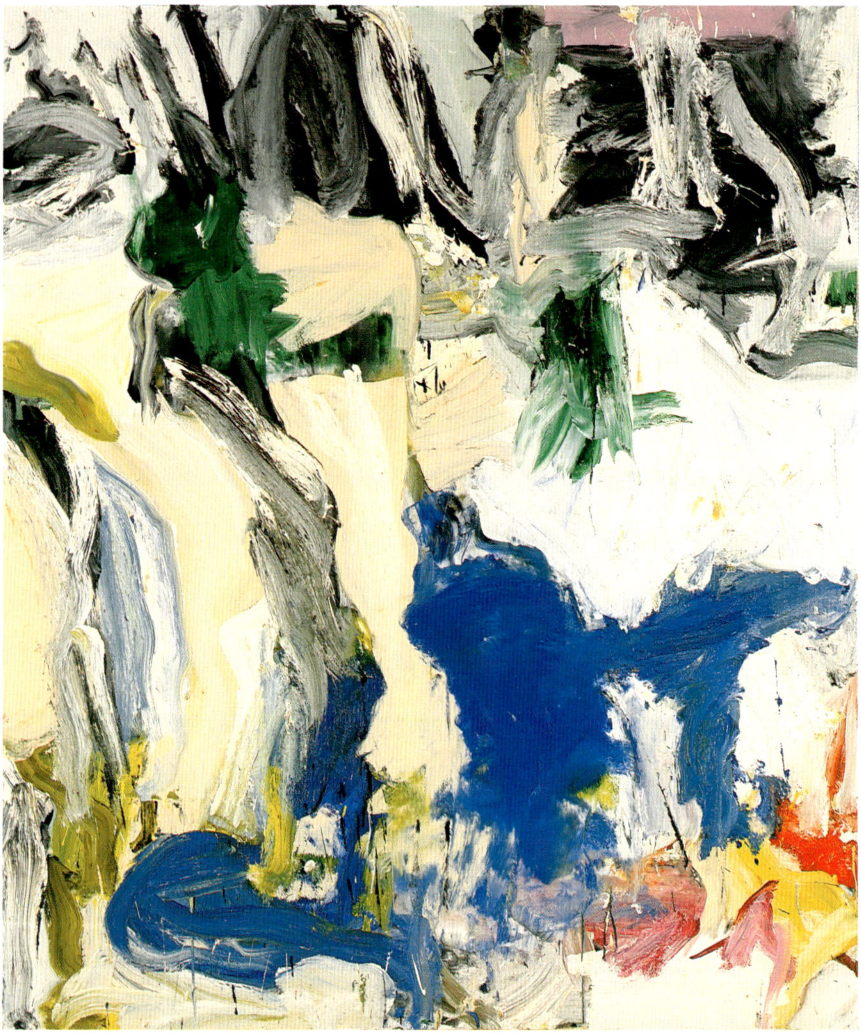

Willem de Kooning
The Netherlands/United States b.1904
Two trees on Mary Street . . . Amen! 1975
Oil on canvas
203.8 x 177.8cm
Purchased 1985 with the assistance of the Queensland Art Gallery Foundation

Willem de Kooning is one of this century's most consistently innovative and ground-breaking artists. He was a pivotal member of the influential abstract expressionist movement in the United States, which developed a new visual vocabulary that stretched the definition of art to its limits. Two trees on Mary Street . . . Amen! *is one of a series of urban landscapes painted by the artist in the mid 1970s. It is typical of his free-flowing style, using a heavily impastoed, gestural brushstroke to convey a sensory experience rather than a figurative representation of the urban environment.*

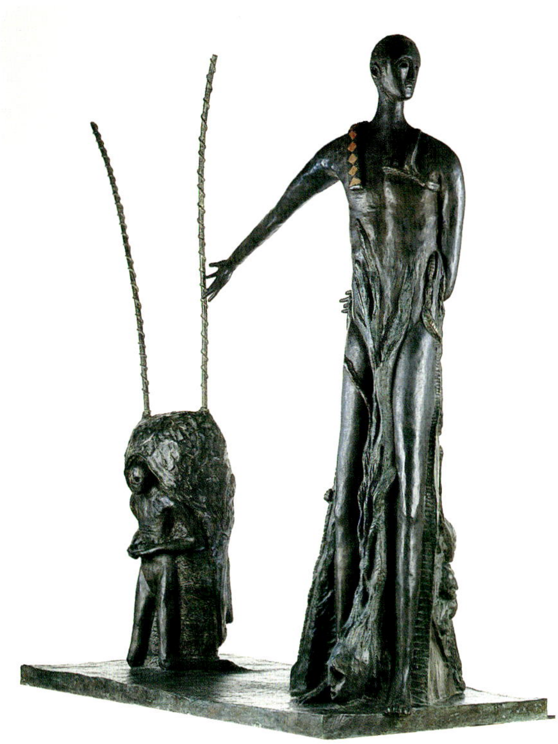

Mimmo Paladino
Italy b.1948
Canto notturno (Night song) 1984
Bronze
ed. 1/3
200 × 230 × 105 cm
Purchased 1985

Mimmo Paladino was born near Benevento in southern Italy, an area rich in archaeological remains from ancient Roman and early Christian times. These cultural traditions have informed the animistic and allegorical symbolism that pervades his work. Canto notturno *combines references from the forces of nature, Graeco-Roman mythology, Christianity and Jungian theories of dreams and symbols, creating an ambiguous narrative that defies concrete interpretation but recalls a wealth of cultural memories.*

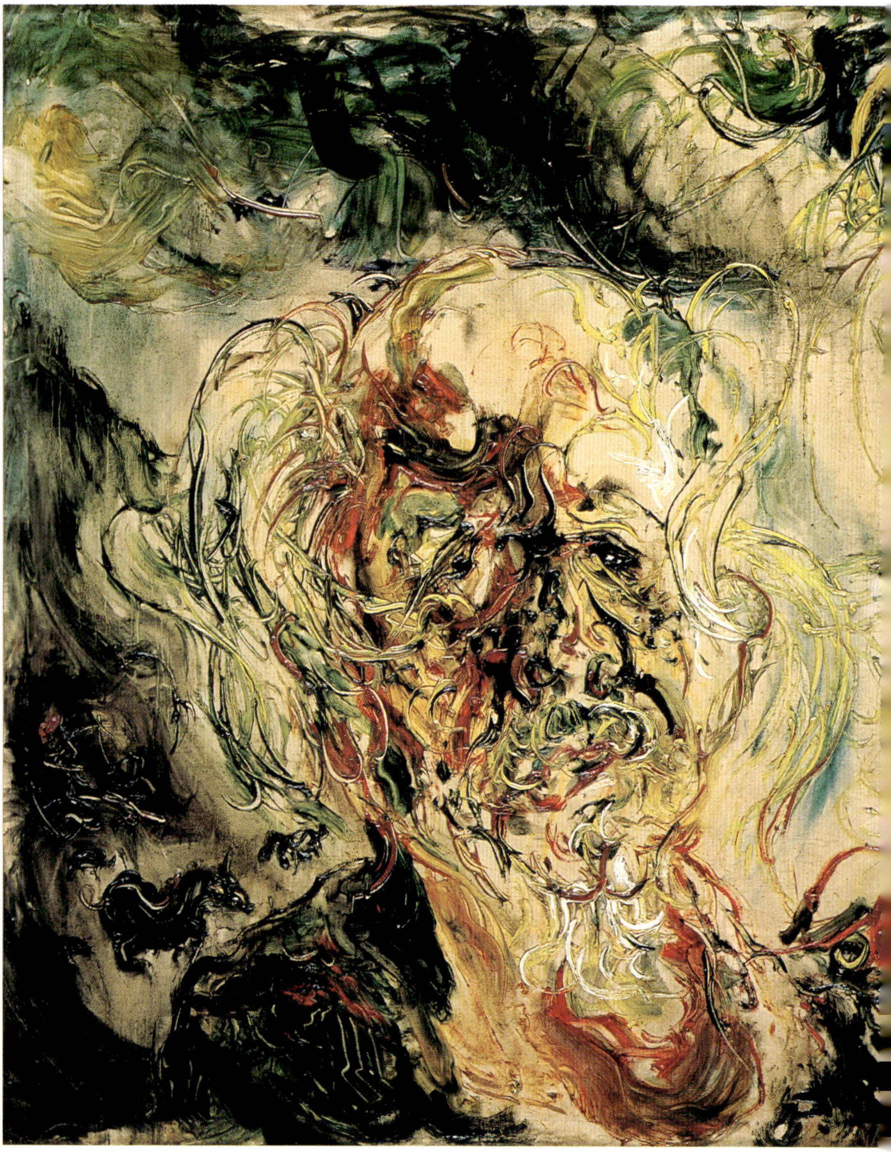

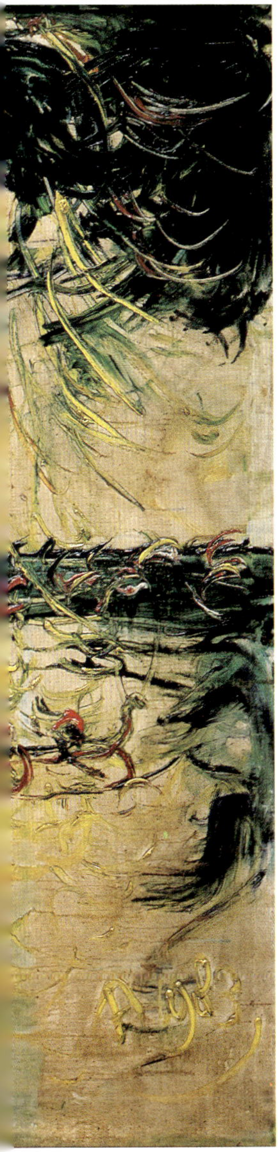

Affandi
Indonesia 1907–90
Self portrait in Kusamba Beach 1983
Oil on canvas
130 x 149.5cm
Purchased 1994 with funds from the International Exhibitions Program. Celebrating the Queensland Art Gallery Centenary 1895–1995

A self-taught artist, Affandi was a driving force in shaping Indonesian contemporary art. During Indonesia's struggle for independence, he eschewed romantic depictions of paradise in favour of images of everyday life created with a stark reality. The self-portrait was a subject to which Affandi frequently turned. Self portrait in Kusamba Beach, *in its free and gestural drawing in paint, is typical of the expressionist style adopted by the artist from the early 1950s.*

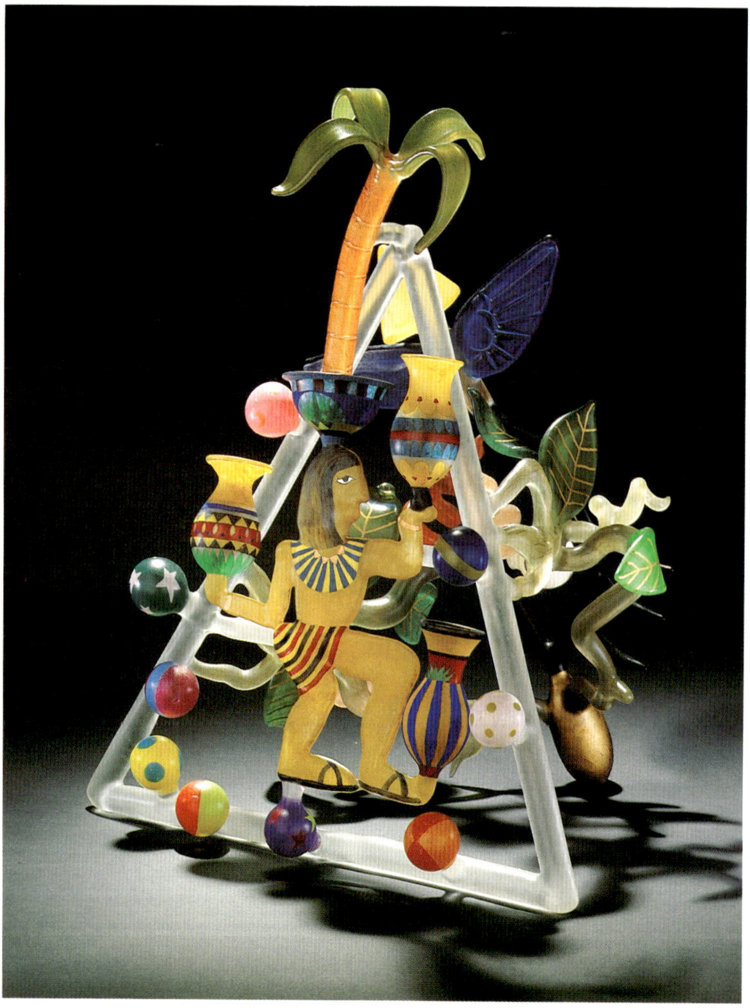

Ginny Ruffner
United States b.1952
The history of juggling in Egyptian gardens 1988
Lampworked and polychrome glass
27 x 32 x 47cm
Purchased 1989

The studio glass movement developed in the United States from the 1950s, but Ginny Ruffner's work is unusual in that she concentrates on lampwork sculptures. She also works on large-scale pieces and public art installations. Her work is humorous and flamboyant, reflecting her curiosity and passion for life. The history of juggling in Egyptian gardens *offers a lighthearted vision of ancient Egyptian culture.*

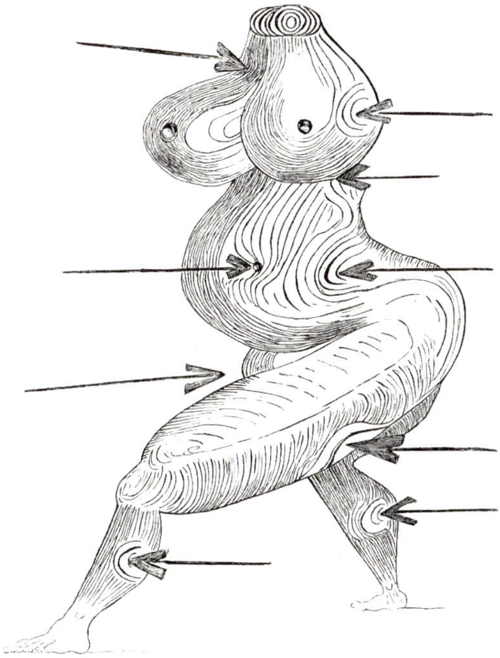

Louise Bourgeois
France/United States b.1911
Sainte Sébastienne 1992
Drypoint
ed. 39/50
98.6 x 78.3cm (comp.)
Purchased 1994 with funds from the 1993 International Exhibitions Program

Although mainly acclaimed for her highly individualistic and personal sculpture, the prints of Louise Bourgeois similarly reflect strong feminist concerns. These often revolve around autobiographical experience and aspects of human emotion such as vulnerability, (sexual) aggression, grief and isolation. In other cases, they are radical reinterpretations of icons of art history. Here, the Christian martyr St Sebastian is transformed into a headless though robust female equivalent. Despite the attacking penetrative arrows, she remains solid and strong.

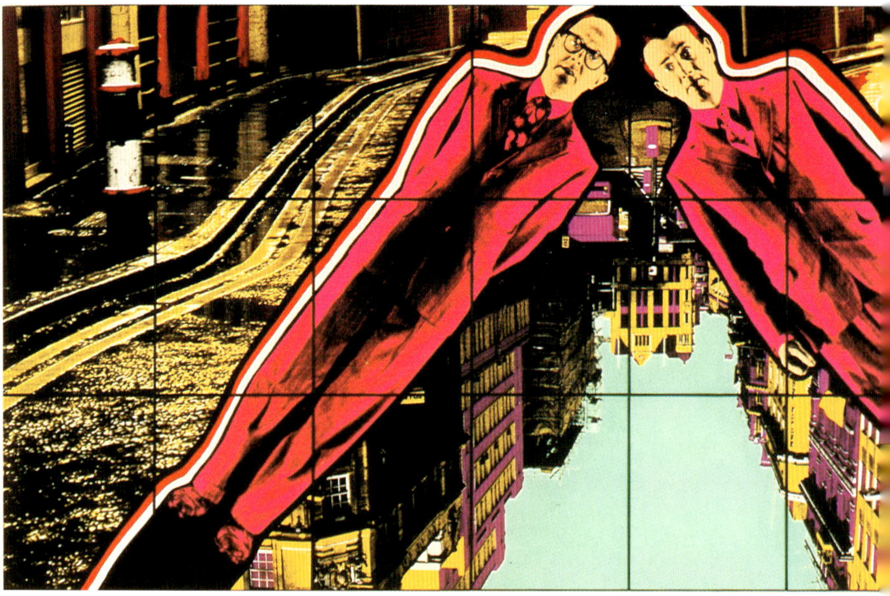

Above
Gilbert & George
England b.1943/1942
Leaners 1989
Type C photograph
24 panels: 253 x 568cm (overall)
Purchased 1994 with funds from the International Exhibitions Program

The collaboration of English artists Gilbert & George began in the late 1960s. They include many aspects of their daily lives in their art, effectively becoming a 'living sculpture'. Their large-scale composite photo-works combine brilliant colour, montage and photogram techniques. Their subjects include an array of socio-political issues with direct relevance to contemporary culture (such as homelessness, alcoholism, homosexuality). Leaners *focuses on the binary character of the world, where nature and man, beauty and ugliness, youth and age are in constant competition.*

Opposite
Cindy Sherman
United States b.1954
Ancienne Manufacture Royale (Limoges)
France est. 1736
Madame de Pompadour née Poisson (1721–1764) 1989
Porcelain with rose Pompadour ground colour, silver and transferred photograph
ed. 25/72
31 x 55.5 x 35cm (complete)
Purchased 1990
Published by Artes Magnus, US

Sherman's photography is unique in that every image is a study of herself assuming a different identity. Madame de Pompadour *was commissioned by Artes Magnus, a group of contemporary art patrons. The artist was asked to design a porcelain table service to be manufactured at the Limoges factory. Sherman chose to decorate a copy of a service made at Sèvres in 1756 for Madame de Pompadour, the mistress of Louis XV of France. Here Sherman inverts the symbol of prestige and power held by Madame de Pompadour by replacing the handpainted portraits of the marquise with screenprinted images of herself.*

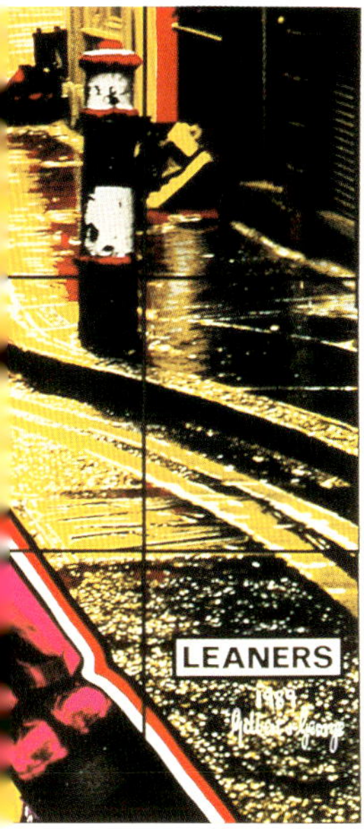
LEANERS
1989

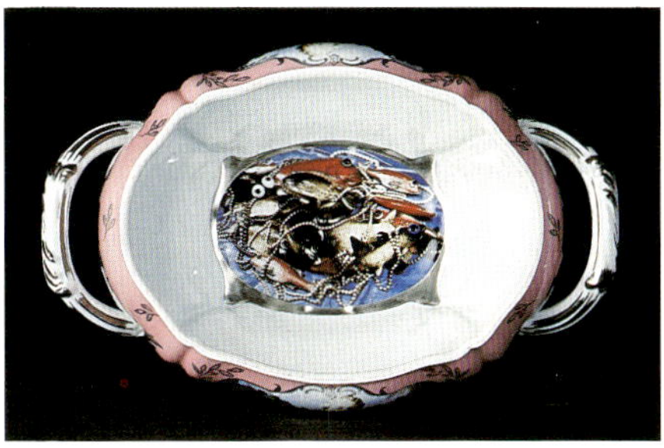

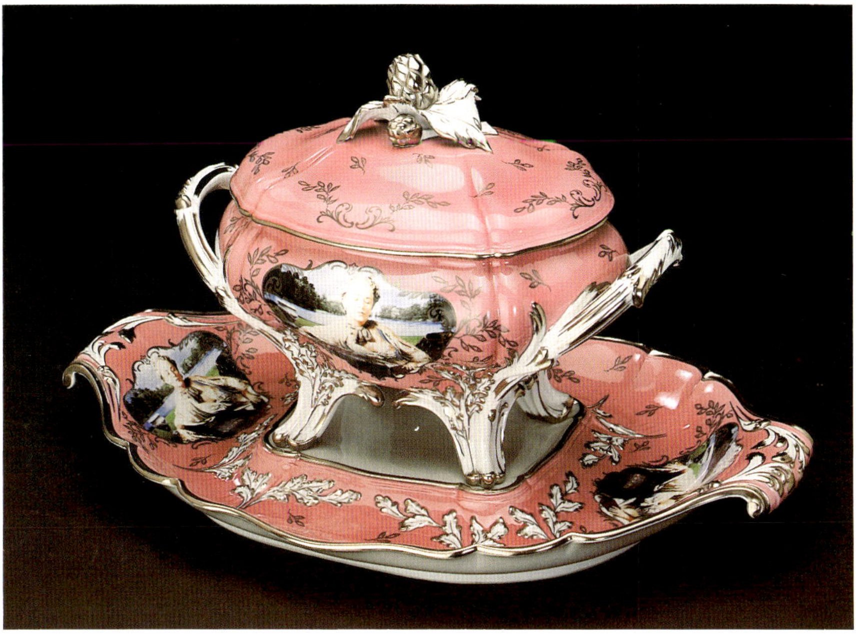

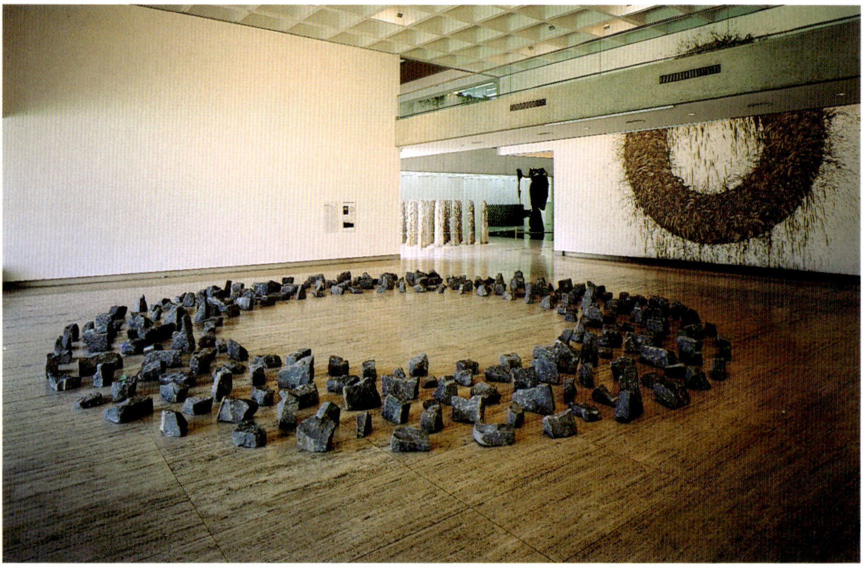

Richard Long
England b.1945
Ring of stones 1982
Installation of 258 stones:
1068cm (diam.)
Purchased 1993 with funds from the International Exhibitions Program

Richard Long's work encompasses a variety of media to record his experiences, both physical and metaphysical, of the natural world. Ring of stones *is an example of Long's installation work in which he uses stones, mud or wood to create circles, spirals or lines that refer to the natural landscape from which the materials are drawn. In such works, Long condenses the vastness of the landscape, and his experience of it, into the Gallery space. He has exhibited internationally since the 1960s.*

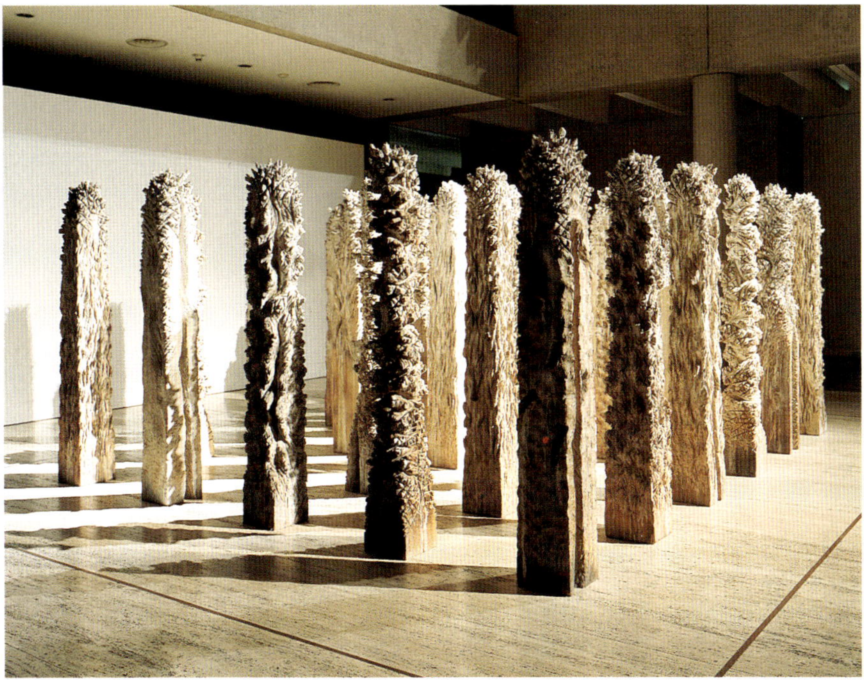

Shigeo Toya
Japan b.1947
Woods III 1991–92
Wood, ash and synthetic polymer paint
Thirty pieces: 220 x 30 x 30cm (each, approx.)
The Kenneth and Yasuko Myer Collection of Contemporary Asian Art. Purchased 1994 with funds from The Myer Foundation, Michael Myer and Ann Gamble Myer through the Queensland Art Gallery Foundation and with the assistance of the International Exhibitions Program

Toya's carved and painted wooden forms represent a highly personal vision of the natural environment through a subtle yet powerful symbolism. One of Japan's most respected contemporary sculptors, his rendering of the landscape and his personal links to it refer not only to the strength and resilience of the natural world, but also to its inherent violence. The artist's work is a search for form which is not preconceived, but becomes apparent during the carving process.

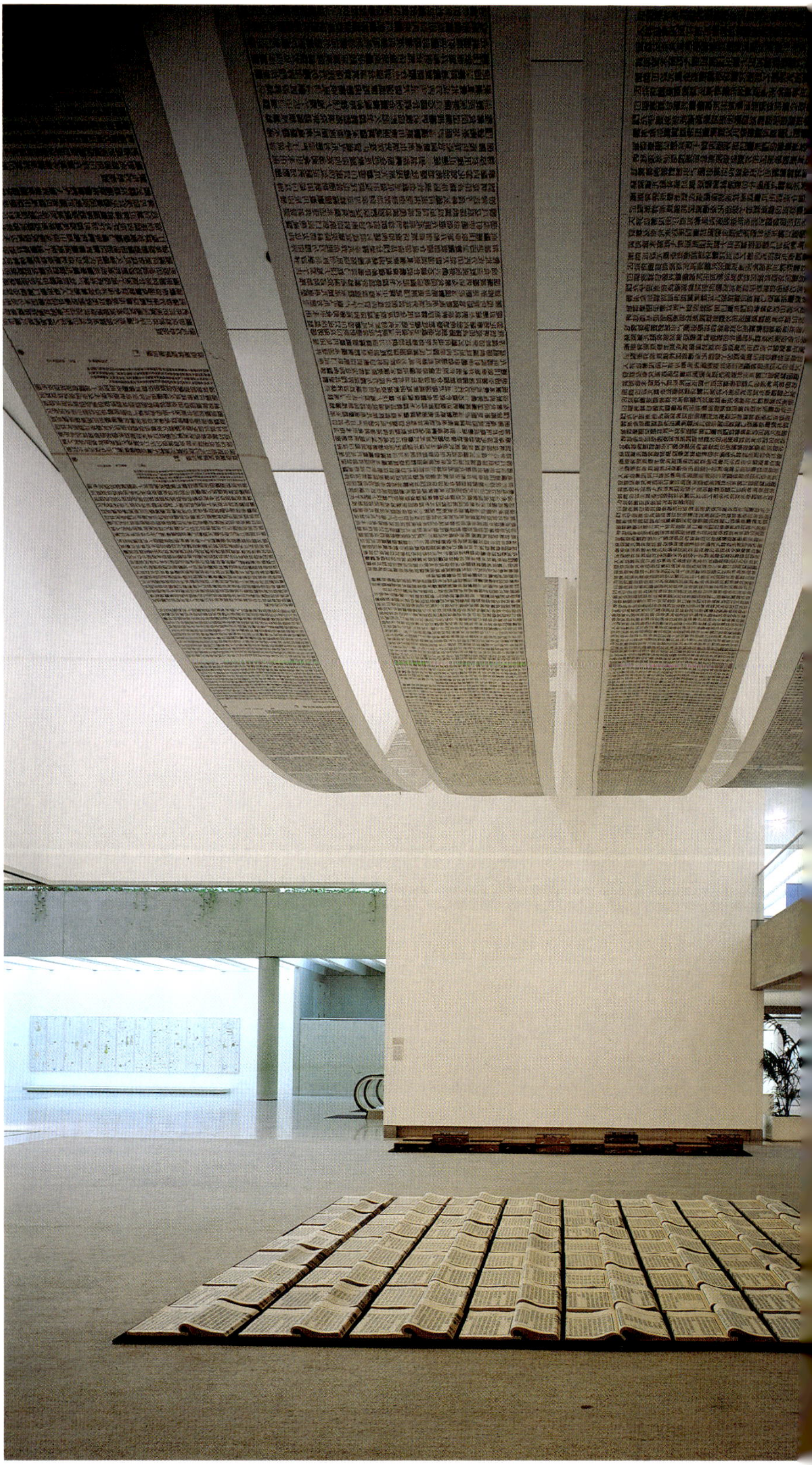

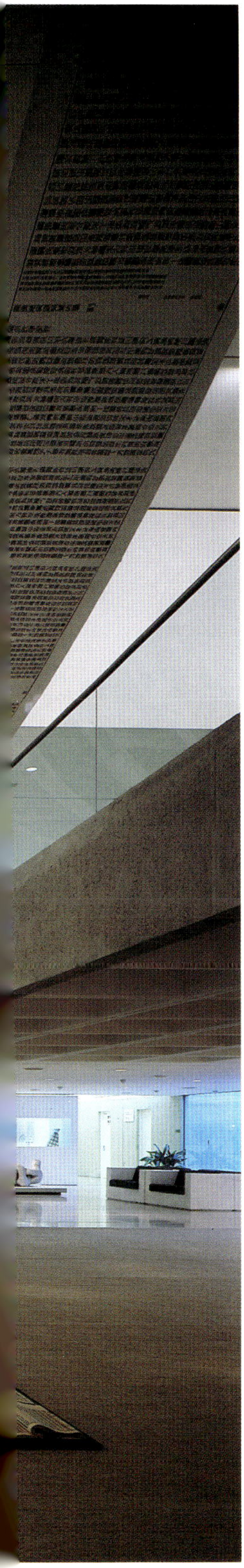

Xu Bing
China/United States b.1955
A book from the sky
1987–91
Installation of printed banners and wooden boxes
The Kenneth and Yasuko Myer Collection of Contemporary Asian Art. Purchased 1994 with funds from the International Exhibitions Program and with the assistance of The Myer Foundation, Michael Myer and Ann Gamble Myer through the Queensland Art Gallery Foundation

A book from the sky *was created over a three-year period by Xu Bing, a woodcut artist and former lecturer in printmaking at the Central Academy of Fine Art in Beijing. Originally named* A mirror to analyse the world, *it is considered to be one of the most significant and imposing works produced in China during the late 1980s. It is a serial work composed of hand-carved signs resembling Chinese characters but which actually have no meaning. The 'characters' have been conceived by the artist using morphological principles and artistic licence. Xu Bing currently lives in South Dakota, USA.*

Index to artists

This index includes references only to works illustrated.

Affandi 127
Ancienne Manufacture Royale 130
Audette, Yvonne 41
Baldessin, George 62
Bennett, Gordon 77
Bing, Xu (see Xu Bing)
Bizen Kilns 95
Boucher, François 104
Bourgeois, Louise 129
Bowers, Stephen 78
Boyd, Arthur 68
Brack, John 83
Brown, Mike 49
Bunduk, Nym 45
Bunny, Rupert 25
Chelsea-Derby 105
Chelsea Porcelain Works 105
Clouston, Alison 74
Conrade Frères (Nevers) 102
Cook, William Delafield 65
Cossington Smith, Grace (see Smith, Grace Cossington)
Crothall, Ross 49
Crowley, Grace 42
Daniels, Dolly Nampijinpa 80
Danko, Aleks 82
Davila, Juan 73
Degas, Edgar 111
de Kooning, Willem 124
Delaunay, Sonia 117
Djulwarak, Dawidi 58
Dobell, William 37
Drew, Marian 79
Drysdale, Russell 35
Dudreville, Leonardo 116
Dupain, Max 38
Dürer, Albrecht 99
Edwards, William 13
Elliott, Judi 78
Erichsen, Conrad 14
Fairweather, Ian 47
Fletcher, Blandford 109
Fox, E. Phillips 27
Fullbrook, Sam 64
Gascoigne, Rosalie 75
Gilbert & George 130
Harvey, L.J. 30
Heidenreich, Mark 78
Heysen, Hans 35
Hiroshige, Ichiryusai 106
Hogarth, Erichsen & Co. 14
Hogarth, Julius 14
Horst, Horst P. 120
Jenner, Isaac Walter 18
Jones, Evan 13
Jonson, Cornelius 103
Kemp, Roger 62
King-Smith, Leah 84
Klippel, Robert 54
Kngwarreye, Emily Kame 81
Kossatz, Les 62
Kunisada II 107
Lahey, Vida 29
Lambert, George W. 26
Lanceley, Colin 49
Levitt, Helen 121
Limoges 130
Lipchitz, Jacques 118
Long, Richard 132
Long, Sydney 23
Mackennal, Bertram 22
Maddock, Bea 66
Marriott, F. Pickford 112
Master of Frankfurt, The 96
Mayo, Daphne 40
Molvig, Jon 46
Mora, Mirka 62
Namatjira, Albert 34
Nevers 102
Nickolls, Trevor 70
Nolan, Sidney 39
Oliver, Bronwyn 86
O'Malley, Glen 66
Ostade, Adriaen van 103
Paladino, Mimmo 125
Parr, Mike 85
Perceval, John 40
Picasso, Pablo 115
Pinton Atelier 117
Proctor, Thea 31
Purves Smith, Peter 36
Rees, Lloyd 34
Riley, Bridget 123
Risley, Tom 74
Rivers, R. Godfrey 20
Robinson, William 69, 91
Rodin, Auguste 110
Rooney, Robert 53
Rowley Gallery 118
Ruffner, Ginny 128
Russell, John Peter 21
Sachs, Bernhard 84
Shepherdson, Gordon 69
Sherman, Cindy 130
Sibley, Andrew 62
Smith, Grace Cossington 43
Spooner, Rodney 88
Soutine, Chaim 119
Stephan, Pierre 105
Streeton, Arthur 28
Swan, James 67
Temin, Kathy 87
Thaiday, Ken 89
Thomas, Rover 80
Tiffany, Louis Comfort 113
Tilson, Joe 122
Tintoretto 100
Toulouse-Lautrec, Henri de 111
Toya, Shigeo 133
Traill, Jessie 30
Tucker, Albert 38
Unknown 14, 17
van Ostade, Adriaen (see Ostade, Adriaen van)
Wakelin, Roland 33
Whiteley, Brett 61
Williams, Fred 57
Withers, Walter 28
Yaxley, William 71
Yirawala 44
Xu Bing 135